T0195815

the ANATOMY of a BIBLICAL Leader

Dan A. Esteline, Sr.

WESTBOW
PRESS®
A DIVISION OF THOMAS NELSON
& ZONDERVAN

WestBow Press books may be ordered through
booksellers or by contacting:

WestBow Press
A Division of Thomas Nelson & Zondervan
1663 Liberty Drive
Bloomington, IN 47403
www.westbowpress.com
1 (866) 928-1240

ISBN: 978-1-9736-7303-3 (sc)
ISBN: 978-1-9736-7302-6 (e)

Library of Congress Control Number: 2019913635

Print information available on the last page.

WestBow Press rev. date: 9/19/2019

ABSTRACT

The subject of the biblical church model (1 Thessalonians 1:1-10) is examined in the introduction. However, the major focus is on the Apostle Paul's attributes of leadership which will be examined in the exegesis of 1 Thessalonians 2:1-12. The goal of this endeavor is not only to identify the attributes by the exegesis of words, phrases and sentences but also to suggest practical applications for each attribute. Technical information is recorded in the footnotes, while the commentary is in the body of the paper. There are Appendices included which address direct application of leadership principles from 1 Thessalonians 2:1-12. Additionally, in the Appendices there are three sermon outlines on 1 Thessalonians 1 and 2 which could be used to instruct a congregation on the subject of leadership.

DEDICATION

Throughout my life significant individuals have poured wisdom into me without my realizing it and thus discipling me toward Christlikeness. No one walks this journey of life without needing the assistance, companionship, encouragement, wisdom, comfort and support of others who walk alongside us at some point in our journey. I acknowledge and dedicate this project to these specific individuals who made the writing and completion of this project possible.

In Memory of:

Sophronia Belle Esterline – my

mother, my dear friend

who became a Christian the same week as

me and during my high school years

together we grew in our Christian lives.

In Memory of:

Rev. Earl H. Harshbarger – my father-

in-law, spiritual example

who as my mentor, teacher and advisor

encouraged me as young pastor.

CONTENTS

Abstract v

Dedication vii

Preface xiii

Introduction to 1 & 2 Thessalonians xvii

Chapter 1: The Manner of a Leader 1

Chapter 2: The Motives of a Leader 17

Chapter 3: The Model of a Leader 41

Appendices

    Appendix #1: Leadership Principles 69

    Appendix #2: Teaching Sermons on
           1 Thessalonians 1 & 2 103

Bibliography 119

PREFACE

Our society today, especially the majority world, pleads for leaders that are visionaries and God-honoring. All of our institutes, families, churches, ministries, businesses and governments are in desperate need of leaders. However, just any leader will not do! These emerging leaders must have the ability to guide and must have character traits that can be trusted, as well as ideas that can be shared and implemented. Therein lies the problem. Many leaders have adopted a definition of leadership that is based on outward success regardless of morals, values or ethics. This kind of leadership exposes the heart as being anything but godly.

The crisis of leadership points to the need for a new style of leadership in the majority world, as well as in the West. The leadership style of the precolonial ruler or "king" will not work in today's context. This style does not fit the context of the growing educated community of the majority world. Paul in 1 Thessalonians 2:1-12 instructs the believers on a style of leadership that is God honoring. As this work is read, it will become obvious that all the attributes of a leader that Paul develops fall under two categories:

- The godly leader should be like a *shepherd*. "The fulfillment such leaders receive does not come from the applause of their followers but from the difference that their service makes in terms of the growth and development of their people."[1]
- The godly leader should also be like a *servant*. "Such leaders demonstrate genuine and selfless motivation. They spend time with their people, get to know them, empower them, and admonish them as needed. And they constantly point to Kingdom values and perspectives."[2]

As this work is read and studied, these two categories should be kept in mind. The leadership style that Paul develops in the 1 Thessalonians passage enables the emerging leader to be both a shepherd and a servant leader.

---

[1] John Jusu, Supervising Editor, *Africa Study Bible* (Wheaton: Oasis International Ltd, 2016), 686.
[2] Ibid., 686.

INTRODUCTION TO 1 & 2 THESSALONIANS

The City of Thessalonica:

1. *The Location:* The city of Thessalonica was a large city in the northern part of Greece. It is believed that during Paul's time the city was a populous of 200,000. Thessalonica was a very wealthy city and the most important one in Macedonia. Further, it was located on a natural harbor on the Aegean Sea, as well as at the juncture of the Via Egnatia (the major east-west highway from Asia Minor all the way to Rome) and the road north to the Danube. Earlier at this location there was a city, Therma or Therme, which may have derived its name from the warm

mineral springs still located at Thessalonica. To the southwestern horizon was Mount Olympus, the home of the Greek gods.

2. *Name:* Thessalonica became important about 315 B.C. when Cassander, the son-in-law of Philip of Macedon, enlarged and strengthened the city. He renamed the city after his wife, the sister-in-law of Alexander the Great. The shortened form of Thessalonica is Salonika, which is the name of the city today.

3. *Political Structure:* "Thessalonica was a free city allowing it to keep its traditional structure of a democratic civil administration, unlike its neighboring communities."[3] There were at least two levels of authority. The lowest level of authority was the citizens who handled public business. The Jews attempted to bring Paul and Silas before this assembly (Acts 17:5). The higher authority was called politarchs who seemed to

have had much more authority than the lower council (Acts 17:6-8).

4. *Inhabitants:* The majority of people living in Thessalonica were Greeks. However, there were also some Romans and Orientals who lived there. "Because of the attractive commerce at Thessalonica, there was a large Jewish colony in the city."[4] It is also believed there were many Gentiles, "God-fearers", who lived in the city. They had left their pagan religion and frequented the synagogue to become proselytes to Judaism. Thessalonica demonstrated a religiously pluralistic environment (cf. 1 Thess. 1:9; Acts 17:4,7). The imperial cult (emperor worship) played a key role in the religious life of the Thessalonians. By having imperial worship the city demonstrated loyalty to the ruling Caesar. However, this caused the believers in Thessalonica to suffer persecution because of their failure to participate in this pagan worship.

The Church in Thessalonica:

1. *Origin:* The narrative for Paul's evangelistic ministry in Thessalonica is recorded in Acts 17:1-9. On his second missionary journey Paul received a vision of a man from Macedonia calling for help. Paul and his missionary team immediately went over to Europe to the city of Philippi. After a series of events, they pushed west about 100 miles to the city of Thessalonica.

2. *Membership:* In Thessalonica Paul first went to the synagogue which was his custom (Acts 17:1,2). He reasoned from the Scripture with the people of the synagogue for three Sabbath days. His message was concerning the death and resurrection of Christ (Acts 17:2,3). Some people believed, with most of them being God-fearing proselytes and a few leading women (Acts 17:4). Most of the Jews, however, were not persuaded. These Jews caused an uproar in the city, going to the house of Jason and attempting to bring

Paul and his missionary team out to the waiting mob! However, they could not find Paul and his missionary team so they took Jason and some brethren before the leaders, accusing them of harboring Paul and his missionary team. They charged Paul with teaching that there was a king other than Caesar. That king was Jesus! The Jews declared that Paul and his missionary team were turning the world upside down which troubled the rulers of the city. After questioning Jason and the brethren, they released them (Acts 17:5-9). As a result of this situation, Paul and his missionary team moved on to Berea by night.

3. *Length of stay:* The text says that Paul reasoned in the synagogue three Sabbath days. If this was the length of his stay, as some say, it would mean Paul and his missionary team ministered about 21 days.[5] Others believe they were there for a longer period of time, even up to two or three months. "Four points favor the longer stay:

a. Paul received at least two financial gifts from Philippi while one hundred miles away in Thessalonica (Phil. 4:16).

b. Paul settled down long enough in Thessalonica to pursue his secular trade (1 Thess. 2:9; 2 Thess. 3:7-10).

c. Paul's familiarity with the people and the extent of his pastoral care indicate a longer stay (1 Thess. 2:7-8).

d. A three-week ministry to Jews would not have allowed Paul enough time to minister to the city's Gentiles, who were evidently the primary recipients of 1 Thessalonians."[6]

4. *Paul's knowledge of the believers' growth and development:* Before Paul describes the characteristics of a leader, he explains the general condition of this congregation in I Thess. 1:3-10. Paul notes three significant qualities in these believers: their "work of faith", their "labor of love"

and finally their "patience of hope". He further develops these qualities with a commendation.

a. Paul explains the believers' "work of faith" as the initial act of faith from which all good works initiate (1 Thess. 1:3a-5). He saw this group of believers as the elect of God. This is probably not referring to individual believers but to the "the church" as being a corporate elected body of believers. This election gives them a special classification as "beloved brethren". The word "beloved" is a perfect participle which means that God's love existed in the past, continues on to the present and into the future.

The genuineness of these believers is seen in the multiple ways the gospel came to them. First, it did not come to them in word only (1 Thess.:5a). Further, they did not receive the gospel that Paul preached in a superficial way, but "in the power and in the Holy Spirit" (1Thess.1:5). The contrast is clear - it was not with eloquent words but was received in the power of the Holy Spirit. This ministry of the Holy Spirit is seen in John 16:7-11 where Jesus tells His disciples He must go away but He will send "the Helper" (Holy Spirit) and when He comes "He will convict the world of sin, and of righteousness, and of judgment". It was by the convicting power of the Holy Spirit that these Thessalonians came to faith in Christ. Additionally, the gospel came "in much assurance", not only to the missionaries, but also to those receiving their message. With the receiving of Christ as personal Savior, there comes "much assurance". These Thessalonians were a legitimate group of born again individuals and Paul was able, with confidence, to explain to them in I Thess. 2:1-12 the anatomy of a biblical leader.

b. Their "labor of love" is the second quality of these believers (1 Thess. 1:3b,8). The word that Paul uses for labor in 1 Thess. 1:3b means "intense labor united with trouble".[7] "Love" in this phrase is the word "ἀγάπης". "This means that which seeks the highest good in the one loved."[8]

Even though the Thessalonian church was a recently planted church, they had a genuine love for their country. In fact, the "example" of these believers "sounded forth" not only to Macedonia and Achaia, the two provinces in ancient Greece, but "in every place" (1 Thess. 1:7-8). Their passion for sharing the gospel is depicted in the very picturesque word "sounded forth". This Greek word "ἐξηχέω" when changed to English characters spells the word "echo". "Thus the picture is of the message of the gospel so stirring the strings of the

Thessalonians' hearts that it reverberated in strong and clear tones to all Greece and everywhere."[9] It was "the word of the Lord" that sounded out and this has direct reference to the gospel message. The phrase "the word of the Lord", with the same meaning, is used in 2 Thess. 3:1. Sharing the message with others is the believers' greatest "labor of love". This demonstrated to Paul that individuals in the congregation were ready for leadership.

c. Their "patience of hope" (1 Thess. 1:3c, 6-7) is the third quality of these believers. The word "patience" ($\mu\nu\eta\mu o\nu\epsilon\acute{u}\omega$) is "a combination of heroic endurance and manly constancy that courageously faces the various obstacles, trials, and persecutions which may befall the believer…".[10] Believers that can stand during times of trials are ones who are ready to start down the path of leadership. These believers received the Word in much afflic-tion, but with joy that had its source in the Holy Spirit (genitive of source). This caused them to be "examples ($\tau\upsilon\pi\acute{o}\omega$). The English word "type" comes from this Greek word meaning "the mark caused by a blow"; then the definition develops to mean "image" or "example".[11] Paul is declaring that these be-lievers were examples for other Christians in Macedonia and Achaia.

It is obvious why Paul thought these believers were ready for leadership. Understanding these qualities helps in the comprehension of 1 Thess. 2:1-12. He con-cludes the first chapter with further confirmations of these qualities of commendation.

These believers' faith was confirmed in that they turned to God from idols. In a culture that was fear-based, living in fear of the many Greek gods, for them to turn to the living God was a very big decision. I served for many years in the fear-based culture of Ethiopia.

The animistic people of that land are extremely afraid of Satan and his demons. But when God works in their lives, by the convicting power of the Holy Spirit, they stand in church, raise their hands to heaven and repeat, "I deny Satan and I accept Christ". This is a direct turning to God from the control of Satan who has controlled them for so many years.

These believers' love was also confirmed in that they were committed to serving the living and the true God. The word "serve" ($\delta o u \lambda \epsilon \acute{u} \omega$) has the meaning "to be a slave, serve, do service".[12] Just as Christ and Paul were called "slaves", so it was with these new believers. They had not only received Christ as Savior but they had moved to the level of dedication to the lordship of Christ. Christ had become their master!

Lastly, their hope was confirmed. They were waiting for the Lord to come from heaven. This word "wait" ($\dot{\alpha} \nu \alpha \mu \acute{\epsilon} \nu \omega$) is a compound word and is literally translated to "wait up". This reminds me of a story my mother told me when I was growing up. My older brother was in the World War II and was missing in action. They received this news by telegram. Sometime later my brother was found alive and he called home to let mom and dad know he was safe and would be home soon. My mom said she turned the porch light on and had all the ingredients in the house for his favorite meal. She sat up in a chair on the sun porch waiting for my brother. She could hardly stand the anticipation of his soon arrival. These believers in Thessalonica had that kind of anticipation for the coming of their Savior. They were not waiting for an event but for a person, their Savior and Lord. This Savior is the deliverer "from" ($\epsilon\kappa$) the wrath that is coming. This seems to be a reference to the coming tribulation called "the great day of His wrath" in Rev. 6:17.

It is not difficult to understand why Paul would take twelve verses in chapter two to explain to these Thessalonians the anatomy of the leader. Therefore, it is very important to carefully analyze these verses because the development of biblical leaders is crucial for the church today. If leaders are going to be developed, it is the Word of God that will give them direction.

The Epistles:

1. *The occasion of the letters:* Paul was writing to the believers in Thessalonica to commend them for their perseverance in persecution. He may have also been answering questions that Timothy brought back with him after visiting the church. It does appear that this is a possibility (cf. 1 Thess. 4:9; 5:1). Paul also addressed issues the church was facing: the accusations that he had impure motives; that he had not returned to visit the believers because he was a coward; and the laziness and moral laxity of some of the church members, etc.

2. *Place and date of writing:* Paul wrote 1 and 2 Thessalonians from Corinth, cf. Acts 17 & 18. Conservative scholars date the book between A.D. 50 and 51.[13]

3 Arnold E. Clinton, ed., "1 Thessalonians" *Zondervan Illustrated Bible Backgrounds Commentary, Vol.3* (Grand Rapids: Zondervan, 2002), 406.

4 D. Edmond Hiebert, *An Introduction to the Pauline Epistles* (Chicago: Moody Press, 1954), 36.

5 James Everett Frame, *First and Second Thessalonians: The International Critical Commentary.* (Edinburgh: T & T Clark, 1912), 7.

6 John Walvoord and Mark Hitchcock, *1&2 Thessalonians.* (Chicago: Moody Press, 2012), 14.

7 "κοπος": Thayer's *Greek-English Lexicon of the New Testament*, Public Domain, Accordance electronic ed. 12.3.0.

8 Charles Caldwell Ryrie, *First & Second Thessalonians* (Chicago: Moody Press, 1959) pp. 26-27.

9 Ibid., 27.

10 D. Edmond Hiebert, *The Thessalonian Epistles* (Chicago: Moody Press, 1971), 47.

11 "τοπόω": Thayer's *Greek-English Lexicon of the New Testament*, Public Domain, Accordance electronic ed. 12.3.0.

12 "δουλεύω": Thayer's *Greek-English Lexicon of the New Testament*, Public Domain, Accordance electronic ed. 12.3.0.

13 John Walvoord and Mark Hitchcock, *1&2 Thessalonians, 13.*

CHAPTER 1

THE MANNER OF A LEADER

I THESSALONIANS. 2:1,2

1 Thessalonians 2:1

"For you yourselves know, brethren, that our coming to you was not in vain."[14]

"Αὐτοὶ[15] γὰρ οἴδατέ[16] ἀδελφοί,τὴν εἴσοδον ἡμῶν τὴν πρὸς[17] ὑμᾶς ὅτι οὐ κενὴ[18] γέγονεν,"

It goes without saying that any leader who considers himself a believer, and/or a Christian, will want the power of the Holy Spirit in their life. Before the potential leader takes a careful look at 1 Thess. 2:1-12, they need to understand something of the presence and power of the Holy Spirit in the life of the believer. This presence and power of the Holy Spirit requires living in fellowship with God, confessing sins on a daily basis and knowing that God forgives and cleanses from all unrighteousness, cf. I John 1:9. The word "confess" (ὁμολογέω) means "to speak the same, to agree". When true confession is made, the same thing is being said about sin that God says and the individual is forgiven. In relationship to the Holy Spirit's power in the life of a believer, Lewis Sperry Chafer outlined it using the following three imperatives:

- "Quench not," (I Thess. 5:19): "Do not quench the Spirit." The word "quench" (σβέννυμι) means "to extinguish, do not stop the activity of the Spirit". Therefore, the leader must be open to the leading of the Holy Spirit in their leadership role. Their role is not about themselves but about God and His plan.

- "Grieve not," (Eph. 4:30): "And do not grieve the Holy Spirit of God." The word "grieve" (λυπέω) means "to cause someone to be sad, sorrowful, or distressed". Paul must surely be writing of the

2

possibility of the leader to be disobedient, thus living in sin.

- "Walk in," (Gal. 5:16): "I say then: Walk in the Spirit, and you shall not fulfill the lust of the flesh." "If we live in the Spirit, let us also walk in the Spirit" (Gal. 5:25). When Paul writes of "walking in the Spirit" (πνεύματι περιπατεῖτε), he is describing "to live or behave in a customary manner, with a possible focus upon the continuity of action — 'to live, to behave, to go about doing' ".[19] "That the righteous requirement of the law might be fulfilled in us who do not walk according to the flesh but according to the Spirit." (Romans 8:4).[20]

Before the leader can be concerned about results in the ministry that God has given them, they must be sure that they are coming with pure motives. The motive of ministry must be first about the glory of God and doing His will. When that is the heart of the leader, the ministry will be all about God and very little about themselves. Then the leader will say with the apostle

Paul, "Therefore, whether you eat or drink, or whatever you do, do all to the glory of God" (1Cor. 10:31). The apostle Paul will have more to say about motives in ministry later in this passage.

This is not to say that the leader is not to be concerned about results, but when the motives are pure the credit for productivity will quickly be attributed to God. When this happens, the ministry will have first and foremost an upward look. For example, James wrote in his epistle, "Every good gift and every perfect gift is from above, and comes down from the Father of lights, with whom there is no variation or shadow of turning" (James 1:17). When results are contemplated in a goal orientated ministry, the good-to-great framework of Jim Collins in his book *Good to Great* should be considered. His monograph, *Good to Great and the Social Sectors,* lays out this framework as follows:

- **Disciplined People**
  -Level 5 Leadership   Getting things done
  within a diffuse
  power structure.

-First Who, then What   Getting the right people on the bus, within the social (ministry) constraints.

- **Disciplined Thought**
  -Confront the Brutal Facts
  -The Hedgehog Concept   The hedgehog concept – rethinking the economic engine without a profit motive.

- **Disciplined Action**
  -Culture of Discipline
  -The Flywheel   Turning the flywheel – building momentum by building the brand.

- **Building Greatness to Last**
  -Clock Building, not Time Telling
  -Preserve the Core / Stimulate Progress[21]   You must retain faith that you can prevail to greatness in the end, while retaining the discipline to confront the brutal facts of your current reality.

1 Thessalonians 2:1 emphasizes that the apostle came to this city with pure motives and a very clear strategic plan to have results all for the glory of God. This interpretation takes in to account both meanings of the word "vain" (κενη). (cf. footnote 18)

1 Thessalonians 2:2

"But even after we had suffered before and were spitefully treated at Philippi, as you know, we were bold in our God to speak to you the gospel of God in much conflict."

ἀλλὰ προπαθόντες καί ὑβρισθέντες[22] καθὼς οἴδατε ἐν Φιλίπποις ἐπαρρησιασάμεθα[23] ἐν τῷ θεῷ ἡμῶν λαλῆσαι πρὸς ὑμᾶς τὸ εὐαγγέλιον τοῦ θεοῦ ἐν πολλῷ ἀγῶνι.[24]

There are several statements made in 1 Thess. 2:2 that are practical instructions for the leader's development. Persecution, in many parts of the world, is usually a part of being a godly leader. It can be slander, insults, or physical in nature. Regardless of how it comes, boldness/courage is a character trait of the leader that is used of God. In almost every city where Paul and his missionary team ministered, they were called to be courageous.

This was true as well in the Old Testament. Consider Moses when God asked him to go before Pharaoh and speak on His behalf (Exod. 3:10). Immediately Moses responded, "Who am I that I should go to Pharaoh, and that I should bring the children of Israel out of Egypt?" (Exod. 3:11). Throughout the third and fourth chapters of Exodus, Moses makes excuses why he cannot lead the people of Israel out of Egypt. Finally, after God gave Moses signs that He would be with him, Moses declares one last excuse, "O my Lord, I am not eloquent, neither before nor since You have spoken to Your servant, but I am slow of speech and slow of tongue" (Exod. 4:10). God made it clear that He would be with Moses but still he made excuses. Finally, the anger of the LORD was kindled against him but God still used the mouths of both Moses and Aaron (Exod. 4:11ff). Clearly Moses' difficulty was a lack of trust in his God, thus leaving him without the courage to obey what God was asking him to do! The lessons are many from this Old Testament story. However, the paramount lesson is that courage (trust in God) is necessary to lead God's people. Perhaps all the excuses that Moses made were true, but that was not the issue. God will never call the leader to do anything that He will not equip them to do! Is it any wonder when Joshua was being prepared to lead the children of Israel into Canaan, God would declare to him, "Be strong and of good courage…Only be strong and very courageous…" (Josh. 1:6,7).

The leader's courage should be like that of the Apostle Paul. Just as Paul was, the leader is called to be courageous in their sharing of the gospel. If those who do statistical analysis are correct, most Christians don't share the gospel with any regularity. It is easy to hide in the church community never really engaging with unbelievers in any meaningful relationship. However, if the leader is going to be an example to those they serve, they must be "bold" to share the wonderful words of life. For our brothers and sisters in the majority world that could mean being bold to share in spite of persecution. All leaders should subscribe to the Voice of the Martyrs' free monthly periodical or email, which will enable them to pray intelligently for the greater Christian community.

This is not to say that Christian leaders in the rest of the world will not go through persecution. It seems persecution comes when believers stand for biblical ethics, values and theology. If Christian leaders are to live by biblical ethics, values and theology, they will need to revisit the Sermon on the Mount. Even for those who see this as the manifesto of the future kingdom, the principles are applicable to all people in every age. I would draw the readers' attention to Dr. Scott McKnight's book entitled *The Story of God Bible Commentary: Sermon on the Mount.*[25] In his book, Dr. McKnight looks at Jesus' ethics as a combination of ethics from Above (Torah), Beyond (Prophets), and Below (Writings). Ethics and values are two of the major problems in leadership today. It takes courage to take a stand on moral issues, to be impeccably honest and to stand as a person of integrity, as well as one sharing the gospel. "The people of South Sudan say that a man who cannot make a decision is holding the stick in the middle."[26] The leader must be courageous and grab God's end of the stick!

Additionally, for many leaders, theology has become ambiguous. Systematic theology is not taught from many pulpits. Modern day issues of theology, such as what is the gospel, what about spiritual gifts, the extent of the atonement, the Islamic view of God, etc. are not being addressed.

Paul stated he was bold to speak the gospel; therefore, leaders should be concerned with "What is the gospel?". The best place to find the answer to this question is in John's Gospel which was written for that purpose. "And truly Jesus did many other signs in the presence of His disciples, which are not written in this book; but these are written that you may believe that Jesus is the Christ, the Son of God, and that believing you may have life in His name" (John 20:30,31). Just a cursory look at John's Gospel makes it clear that the only condition of salvation is receiving Jesus Christ by faith. One of the clearest accounts is Jesus encounter with Martha in John 11. Martha's brother Lazarus had died and she was wondering why Jesus had not come sooner. If He had, she thought, her brother would not have died (John 11:21). Jesus went on to explain that her brother would rise again. Martha was aware of this truth for she said, "I know that he will rise again in the resurrection at the last day" (John11:24). Immediately Jesus presented the gospel to her saying: "I am the resurrection and the life. He who believes in Me, though he may die, he shall live. And whoever lives and believes in Me shall never die. Do you believe this?" (John 11:25,26). Martha affirms that she is a believer and her affirmation is very clear: "Yes, Lord, I believe that You are the Christ, the Son of God, who is to come into the world" (John 11:27). Martha believed two things: Jesus was the Christ (Messiah) and that He was deity (Son of God). To put this same gospel in Pauline terms we read:

"Moreover, brethren, I declare to you the gospel which I preached to you, which also you received and in which you stand, by which also you are saved, if you hold fast that word which I preached to you—unless you believed in vain. For I delivered to you first of all that which I also received: that Christ died for our sins according to the Scriptures, and that He was buried, and that He rose again the third day according to the Scriptures…" (1 Cor.15:1-4).

It takes courage to preach a "free grace" gospel when so many individuals are adding a variety of conditions to salvation. Care must be taken not to confuse salvation and sanctification (discipleship). The great commission has two very distinct parts, "And He said to them, 'Go into all the world and preach the gospel to every creature'" (Mark 16:15). It is the preaching of the gospel, by the power of the Holy Spirit, that brings individuals to a saving knowledge of Jesus Christ. And consider, the second part of the great commission found in Matt. 28:19-20: "Go therefore and make disciples of all the nations, baptizing them in the name of the Father and of the Son and of the Holy Spirit, teaching them to observe all things that I have commanded you; and lo, I am with you always, even to the end of the age. Amen." This is sanctification - "making disciples"! Earl Radmacher in his book *Salvation* has a chart that clearly shows the past, present, and future of the salvation story.[27]

---

[14] Unless otherwise indicated, all Scripture quotations are taken from the New King James Version© (NKJV) Copyright 1982 by Thomas Nelson, Inc.

[15] Unless otherwise indicated, all Greek Scripture quotations are taken from *The Greek New Testament*© Copyright 2017 by Crossway.

[16] "The people in the provinces talk about it far and wide, they have only heard the story, *you* are the ones who *know.*" R.C.H. Lenski, *The Interpretation of St. Paul's Epistles to the Colossians, to the Thessalonians, to Timothy, to Titus and to Philemon* (Minneapolis: Augsburg Publishing House, 1937), p.238. "For you yourselves know" (Αὐτοι γὰρ οἴδατε). "For" (γάρ) is usually a particle that links a statement with what has immediately preceded but in this verse it connects the reader with 1 Thess. 1:9. "You yourselves" is in the emphatic position making it clear that Paul, Silvanus, and Timothy are declaring the believers at Thessalonica to be the proof of their ministry because they experienced it.

[17] "Their coming" (ἀδελφοί,τὴν εἴσοδον ἡμῶν τὴν πρὸς) is not a reference to their initial arrival but rather the entire time they had ministered among them.

[18] What the believers knew was the apostles' ministry among them was not in "vain" (κενή). This word "vain" can mean either "pertaining to being without anything — 'empty, empty-handed.'" Or "pertaining to lacking in results — 'without result, without effect.'" Johannes P. Louw & Eugene A. Nida "κενη" *Greek-English Lexicon of the New Testament Based on Semantic Domains*, Accordance electronic ed. 12.3.0 (New York: United Bible Societies, 1988, 1989), p.786. Lenski contends the first definition of "empty or

hollow" is the meaning in this context (Ibid.). The first meaning would put emphasis on the character of their ministry, cf. 1 Cor.15:14; Eph. 5:6; Col.2:8; Jas.2:20. This would be affirming the apostles' motives as being pure. Phillips and Moffatt support the other meaning which puts the emphasis on the results of their ministry that it was "not a failure", cf. 1 Cor.15:10, 58; 2 Cor.6:1. Green's summary is instructive when he writes, "While the primary emphasis appears to be on the apostolic mission, the missionary character was bound up with the results of the mission." Gene L. Green, *The Letters to the Thessalonians* (Grand Rapids: William B. Eerdmans Publishing Company, 2002), p.115. I believe it is best to understand that the apostles came to the believers in the power of the Holy Spirit, with pure motives and with a specific purpose.

[19] Johannes P. Louw & Eugene A. Nida "περιπατέω" *Greek-English Lexicon of the New Testament Based on Semantic Domains*, Accordance electronic ed. 12.3.0 (New York: United Bible Societies, 1988, 1989), 506.

[20] Lewis Sperry Chafer, *He That is Spiritual* (Wheaton: Van Kampen Press, 1918), Chs. 4,5,6.

[21] Jim Collins, *Good to Great and the Social Sectors*, Monograph, 2005, 8.

[22] The transitional conjunction "but (ἀλλὰ) indicated a strong positive contrast with the previous negative phrase; the visit was not "empty", it was with power and courage to preach the gospel even when they had previously suffered in the hostile environment of Philippi, cf. Acts16:19-40. The apostle, at this juncture, does not show a contrast leading to results but he is again revealing that the missionary team's ministry was with pure motives. Evidently, their genuine and pure motives were so transparent that Paul states "as you know" (καθὼς οἴδατε). Their persecution came in two forms of "suffering" (προπαθόντες). This word refers to physical suffering and specifically to flogging and having their feet in stocks. The words "spitefully treated" (ὑβρισθέντες) refers to being treated with insults from others. Specifically, in this situation, it refers to being slandered, stripped of their clothes, publicly beaten and imprisoned. If they were not possessing genuine and pure motives coupled with courage, they would not have been able to tolerate this kind of treatment. They would have appealed to the fact that they had Roman citizenship.

[23] In spite of all this persecution in Philippi they were "bold" (ἐπαρρησιασάμεθα/ παρρησιάζομαι: to have courage or boldness in the face of danger or opposition — 'to be bold, to have courage.'). They were not bold in themselves but in their God. This means they were able to speak boldly with help from their God. The Greek phrase ἐν τῷ θεῷ (before God) more than likely has the idea Paul was bold not only in the presence of people but before God as well.

[24] This was seen in their willingness to speak the "gospel" (εὐαγγέλιον/good news) "in much conflict" (ἐν πολλῷ ἀγῶνι /Johannes P. Louw & Eugene A. Nida "ἀγῶνι" "danger or opposition" *Greek-English Lexicon of the New Testament Based on Semantic)* Accordance electronic ed. 12.3.0. (New York: United Bible Societies, 2011).

[25] Scot McKnight, *The Story of God Bible Commentary: Sermon on the Mount* (Grand Rapids: Zondervan, 2013), 8-13.

[26] John Jusu, Supervising Editor, *Africa Study Bible*, 1122.

[27] Earl D. Radmacher, *Salvation* (Nashville: Thomas Nelson Publishers, 2000), 6.

SO GREAT SALVATION

FREE GIFT	PROCESS	EVALUATION
As a result of trusting Christ	of abundant	to determine reward
For Salvation (Jn. 3:16; Rom. 3:24; Rev. 22:17)	growth/maturity (Jn. 10:10; Phil. 2:12; 2 Pet. 1:5-9)	(Mt. 16:24-27; 1Cor. 4:5; 2 Cor. 5:10; Col. 3:23-25; Rev. 3:21; 22:12)
Theological: Justification	**Theological: Sanctification**	**Theological: Glorification**
Offer: Whoever	Offer: Christ's Disciples	Offer: All believers
Basis: Faith alone in Christ	Basis: Faith resulting in Obedience	Basis: Faithful obedience
Description: Free gift	Description: Works, deeds, degrees	Description: Various
How often: One time	How often: Lifetime process	How often: One time (Judgment seat of Christ)

CHAPTER 2

THE MOTIVES OF A LEADER

I THESSALONIANS 2:3-6
(CHARACTERISTICS TO OMIT)

1 Thessalonians 2:3

"For our exhortation *did* not *come* from error or uncleanness, nor *was it* in deceit."

"Ἡ γὰρ παράκλησις²⁸ ἡμῶν οὐκ ἐκ πλάνης²⁹, οὐδὲ ἐξ ἀκαθαρσίας³⁰, οὔτε ἐν δόλῳ³¹."

In verses 3-6, Paul appeals to the Thessalonian believers concerning characteristics that were not part of his missionary team's motives; characteristics that must be omitted from a godly leader. Paul's appeal was not just an intellectual argument but also a reaching out to the emotional side of the believer's being. As leaders, Paul and his missionary team were extremely careful not to use their education as permission to usurp authority in leading people in the direction that they wanted them to go! The content of their appeal was not just an emotional appeal, but an appeal free of error. The Greek preposition "ἐκ", translated "from", means "out of" and points to the origin or source; while the Greek negative "οὐκ", translated "not", is used in the denial of the objective fact. Both of these words are used together in this verse to show emphasis.

Paul uses three strong words - "error", "uncleanness" and "deceit" - to deny any false motives attributed to the apostles by the enemy. The first strong word Paul uses is "error". In this context, the word "error" does not refer to deception which would refer to the method of their preaching, but rather "error" in the theology of the gospel message which he faithfully preached. This is another reminder that the believers' understanding of the gospel must be without error. Whatever else, the gospel is God's good news, and therefore cannot have any source of error. The leader must not be so familiar with presenting the gospel message that he says things that are not biblical. I've listened to preachers on different Sundays present the gospel with different content each week. For example, one week they will say, "receive Christ as your Savior and you will be a Christian". The next week they will say, "If you repent of all your sins and accept Christ you will be a Christian". Then the final week they will say, "If you accept Christ as your Savior and commit everything to Him you can be a Christian". I often think - "how confusing, which one of these presentations is true and without error". For the biblical definition of the gospel, the reader is referred back to the comments made on verse two.

The second word Paul uses is "uncleanness". This word could be referring to sexual uncleanness, e.g. sensuality associated with pagan religions. That could indeed be Paul's meaning in this passage. In Thessalonica, the home of his readers, there was notably present the worship of Dioysiacs and the Cabiri. "The character of both of these is indicated by their phallic emblems."[32] However, others believe there are good reasons to reject this view.

1. In classical Greek, it denotes "foulness", "moral foulness", "dirty ways" of a sort.

2. It does not seem to fit well between "error" and "deceit".

3. When Paul elaborates on these characteristics, sexual immorality is not discussed.[33]

It seems what Paul is referring to is "unclean motives". Of course, one must ask which motives? This subject of motives is an important one in leadership. Leaders have been known to have a variety of hidden agendas. Paul, in Phil. 1:14-19, reminds a leader not to preach the right message with the wrong motives. For example, there were those in Philippi who were preaching correctly but with a hidden agenda; "from envy and strife...the former preach Christ from selfish ambition, not sincerely, supposing to add affliction to my chains"

(Phil.1:15b-16). Paul will go into more depth concerning this subject in 1 Thess. 2:4-5. It is sufficient to say the leader should be examining their motives regularly to see if their service is for the glory of God! "Therefore, whether you eat or drink, or whatever you do, do all to the glory of God" (1 Cor. 10:31).

The last word Paul uses to defend his exhortation is "deceit". This is the idea of "trickery" cf. footnote 31. Paul reminds the Thessalonian believers, that not only were his and the missionary teams' motives pure, but their methods were upright as well. They were without deceit or trickery. Just like at Corinth, they did not try to use persuasive words in order to sell themselves (1Cor. 1:4). The Scripture is very clear that deception is a sin (Mark 7:22; John 1:47; Acts 13:10; Rom. 1:29; 1 Pet. 2:1,22; 3:10). For this reason, leaders should be very careful not to be deceptive in their methods to reach people for Christ (2 Cor.12:16). "In the gospel appeal to the Thessalonians, the message was not false, the motivations were not impure, and the methods were not deceptive. The heralds were not hucksters who hustled these people!"[34]

I Thessalonians 2:4

"But as we have been approved by God to be entrusted with the gospel, even so we speak, not as pleasing men, but God who tests our hearts."

"ἀλλὰ Καθὼς δεδοκιμάσμεθα[35] ὑπὸ τοῦ θεοῦ πιστευθῆναι τὸ εὐαγγέλιον, οὕτως λαλοῦμεν, οὐχ ὡς ἀνθρώποις ἀρέσκοντες, ἀλλὰ τῷ θεῷ τῷ δοκιμάζοντι τὰς καρδίας ἡμῶν."

Paul begins this verse with a strong conjunction "but (ἀλλὰ as opposed to δέ) It might be better translated "on the contrary". Against all the slanderers, Paul will expand his defense by another array of facts. His defense starts with the verb "we have been approved". In the Greek text, this is in the perfect tense. This tense indicates a lasting approval, not something completed. "The word was used in classical Greek with the technical sense to describe the passing of a person being fit for election to a public office."[36] Therefore, in this verse,

Paul is making it clear to his readers that God had approved him and his missionary team. The words "by God" are very important for leadership approval, also it is useful to have the approval of man. But, if it comes down to either or, God's approval must be first and foremost in the leader's life. Paul called the churches to examine their leaders (Rom. 14:18; 2 Cor. 13:7; 1 Tim. 3:10) and, then with the churches' approval, individuals should be given responsibility (1 Cor. 16:3; 2 Cor. 8:22). The phrase "…to be entrusted with the gospel" is explanatory, serving to define more clearly to whom the approval was directed. The passive voice of the infinitive ($\pi\iota\sigma\tau\epsilon\upsilon\theta\hat{\eta}\nu\alpha\iota$), "entrusted", indicates that their ministry was a trust given to them by God. Since God chose Paul and his missionary team for this ministry of proclaiming the precious message of the gospel, they had clear responsibility to make sure the gospel message was unadulterated, especially with works! In 1 Cor. 9:17,18, Paul called this responsibility a "stewardship". "For if I do this willingly, I have a reward; but if against my will, I have been entrusted with a stewardship. What is my reward then? That when I preach the gospel, I may present the gospel of Christ without charge, that I may not abuse my authority in the gospel" (cf. Gal. 2:7; 1 Tim. 1:11-12; Titus 1:3).

Interestingly, it is not known for sure when God entrusted Paul and his missionary team with the gospel. The epistle to the Galatians might shed light on this question. It could have been during Paul's time of testing for three-years in Arabia (Gal. 1:16-18). It is clear from Galatians that Paul was chosen even before his birth for the ministry (service) of preaching the gospel, especially to the Gentiles (Gal. 1:15-16).

Leaders should be reminded of the seriousness of being entrusted with the gospel. They must have their soteriology (doctrine of salvation) biblically correct! A common unbiblical teaching today is what is called "Lordship Salvation". [37] This view defines salvation as not only believing in Christ as Savior but also, at the time of believing, an individual must repent of his sins and submit to the lordship of Christ. The "Free Grace" position, which this author espouses, holds that "saving faith is the belief in Jesus Christ as the Son of God who died and rose again to pay one's personal penalty for sin and the One who gives eternal life to all who trust Him and Him alone for it."[38]

Paul now moves on in the text to the subject of who the leader must please, "not as pleasing men, but God who tests our hearts". It seems that leaders in our generation are very concerned about pleasing people they serve. This may come from their strong desire to be people orientated. Of course, the leader does need to have a servant's heart (Matt. 20:25-27). However, Paul was in no way saying that he somehow was going to be displeasing to people (Rom. 15:1-3; 1 Cor. 9:22; 10:33). That being said, quite often what people want and what they need may be two very different things. "The point is rather that the fundamental motivation in their ministry was to please God rather than people (Gal.1:10; 2 Tim. 2:4)."[39] Therefore, the leader must engage in the role of leadership with the very distinct purpose of pleasing God, thus the phrase "not as pleasing men, but God who tests our hearts". At all times, the leader must remember it is God first and foremost who they serve and it is God who choses, tests, approves and commissions them (2 Tim. 2:4). Further, the word "test" ($\delta o \kappa \iota \mu \acute{\alpha} \zeta o \nu \tau \iota$), cf. footnote 35, is a present participle that could be translated "who is testing…". This means that God continues to examine the leader's character in the present and will continually examine the integrity of His messenger. By stating that God examines the heart, Paul means He examines where no human can see (Heb. 4:13).

The practical applications from this verse are obvious but the thrust of this verse is to teach that biblical leadership is from the inside out! God is more concerned with "being" than "doing". Therefore, the leader must continually be examining their own integrity and motives. They must not be leaders who honor God with their lips and whose hearts are far from Him (Mark 7:6).

1 Thessalonians 2:5

"For neither at any time did we use flattering words, as you know, nor a cloak for covetousness—God *is* witness."

"Οὔτε γάρ ποτε ἐν λόγῳ κολακείας[40] ἐγενήθημεν[41]. καθώς οἴδατε,οὔτε ἐν προφάσει πλεονεξίας[42] Θεὸς μάρτυς."

In the Greek New Testament, this verse begins with an explanatory "for" (γάρ). The Thessalonian believers knew without a shadow of a doubt that Paul and his missionary team were genuine in their leadership among them. Not only was God their witness, but the Thessalonian church was their witness as well. It is a natural desire of man to be appreciated. However, Paul's word "flattery" does not just mean complimentary words. Rather, it also has the idea of making a favorable impression to manipulate others for selfish advantage. Frame believes that the word carries with it the idea of deception.[43] This was a problem in the early church as it is today. The problem in the early church was people who were attempting to make money by manipulating congregations. The first book of Christian order called *The Didache* gave guidelines for first-century missionaries and the churches that received them. In the section called *The Teaching of the Twelve Apostles,* there are some illuminating instructions.

> "...let every apostle that cometh unto you be received as the Lord. And he shall stay one day and, if need be, the next also, but if he stays three days he is a false prophet. And when the apostle goes forth, let him take nothing save bread, till he reaches his lodging. But if he asks for money, he is a false prophet. If he that comes is a passer-by, succor him as far as you can. But he shall not abide with you longer than two or three days unless there be necessity. But if he be minded to settle among you and be a craftsman, let him work and eat. But if he has not trade, according to your understanding, provide that he shall not live idle among you, being a Christian. But if he will not do this, he is a Christmonger: of such men beware."[44]

Therefore, the leader is worthy of salary from the church but they must avoid becoming consumed with serving primarily for financial gain. The Holy Spirit ministers through leaders but they are to be sincere and impeccable, genuine before man and God! And old Puritan prayer says, "It is my deceit to preach, and pray, and to stir up others' spiritual affections in order to beget commendations, whereas my rule should be daily to consider myself viler than any man in my own eyes…Let me learn… of Paul…Lord, let me lean on thee as he did, and find my ministry thine."[45]

Paul was not finished with the subject of purity in ministry. Next, he tells the Thessalonian believers that he did not have a "cloak for covetousness". The word "cloak", ($\pi\rho o\phi\acute{\alpha}\sigma\epsilon\iota$), denotes something put forward for appearance to conceal what lies behind it. Paul was declaring that he and his missionary team never used a false front. The word "covetousness" ($\pi\lambda\epsilon ov\epsilon\xi\acute{\iota}\alpha\varsigma$) is a word that literally means "a desire to have more". "Greed is the insatiable and excessive desire to have more and more money; it thinks nothing of using another person or another's property to gain its own ends."[46] This could be a very serious problem for leaders ministering in the majority world. Materialism is a very real danger. These leaders have so little and the temptation to want more and more is very much a reality. Everything from western clothes, sophisticated smartphones, etc. can enhance this temptation. None of these things are wrong in and of themselves but, if they become the desire of the heart, they can lead to the leader using a mask to cover up greed.

As seen in the life of the Apostle Paul, there are precautions that he took to keep his ministry pure before God. Paul worked with his own hands while among the Thessalonians and no one could accuse him of greed (1 Thess. 2:9; 2 Thess. 3:8; 1 Cor. 4:12; Acts 20:34). He made sure that his handling of monies from the churches was always upright (2 Cor. 8:20-21) and insisted that all church leaders be above reproach in their financial affairs (1 Tim. 3:3; Titus 1:7). Not everyone followed his example (1 Tim. 6:5; Titus 1:11; Jude 11).

Both the Thessalonians and God Himself bore witness that this missionary team was a missionary team with integrity, "...as you know...God *is* witness". This appeal shows how important it was for Paul and his missionary team to be cleared of any charge of wrong-doing in their ministry. Of course, the Thessalonian believers could only judge the character of the missionaries' conduct and could not know for sure their true motives. So, Paul appealed directly to God who looks on the heart where man only looks on the outward appearance. The LORD said to Samuel, "...For *the LORD* does not *see* as man sees; for man looks at the outward appearance, but the LORD looks at the heart" (1Sam. 16:7). The final word on this matter that should be given to all leaders is, "Be careful! Be careful! Be careful!".

1 Thessalonians 2:6a

"Nor did we seek glory from men, either from you or from others..."

"οὔτε στυντεδ[47] ἐξ ἀνθρώπων δόξαν[48] οὔτε ἀφ
ὑμῶν οὔτε ἀπ' ἄλλων..."

Next, Paul declared they were not looking for praise from the Thessalonian believers or from anyone else. The word "seek" can mean just looking for something but in this context', 8:11-12; Luke 11:16; 12:48; 1 Cor. 1:22; 2 Cor. 13:3)".[49] The phrase "from men" stands in the emphatic position confirming they were not seeking human glory in any sense. "There is a glory which believers rightly seek (Rom. 2:7) but it is not a glory that originates with men. Further, Paul does not deny that he never receives glory from men, or he has no right to it, but he writes that he has sought it 'neither from you,' his Thessalonian converts, 'nor from others,' believers from a distance who had received reports of his work."[50] Who were the "others" in this verse? From the above quote, Hiebert believes that they were Christians in other locations where Paul ministered. However, Green believes that they were "most likely the people in Thessalonica who heard the gospel from Paul and his associates but did not respond to it as did the believers."[51] It seems that Green's view is correct because the whole focus of this passage is upon the missionaries' entrance at Thessalonica (1Thess. 2:1).

The word "glory" ($\delta\acute{o}\xi\alpha\nu$), ($\delta\acute{o}\xi\alpha$) to which Paul was referring, was the honor and prestige that was so common in the philosophical world of his day. The world's philosophy can very easily become a part of the church. Some commentators believe the word "glory" here refers to financial remuneration.[52][53] That "glory" ($\delta\acute{o}\xi\alpha$) ever means a monetary remuneration is questionable. Frame asserts, "There is no evidence that it is equivalent to 'honor' in the later sense of honorarium".[54] Paul wanted the believers at Thessalonica to know that there was no "glory seeking" with him nor his missionary team! "Dio Chrysostom decried those Cynics who would declaim publicly just for the glory they would receive, 'who are lifted aloft as on wings by their fame and disciples'. Dio ridiculed one sophist named Prometheus who was 'being destroyed by popular opinion (doxa); for his liver swelled and grew whenever he was praised and shriveled again when he was censured'."[55]

Importantly then, this negative of "glory seeking" should be a real concern to any leader. If individual leaders are doing a commendable job, they may receive compliments and words of appreciation from the people they lead. There is nothing wrong with this. However, before long they may start seeking the approval of people. This may cause the leader to allow issues to slide because they do not want to point out sin or any wrong-doing for fear that people will no longer appreciate their leadership. It is very easy for the leader to think more highly of himself than he ought to think (Rom. 12:3). So, let the leader be careful! When they receive praise from people, the leader must remember that all they have comes from the Lord and that all they accomplish must be for the glory and honor of the Lord. Our God is a jealous God and He will not share His glory!

1 Thessalonians 2:6b

"...when we might have made demands as apostles of Christ."

"...δυνάμενοι[56] ἐν βάρει[57] εἶναι ὡς Χριστου ἀπόστολοι[58]

The phrase "might have made demands" is quite literally "to be in weight" which Findlay aptly calls "an ambiguous phrase".[59] Again, some believe that this phrase refers to the right to financial support for their work, or it may be understood in a sense of their importance, hence "authority, dignity", pointing to their office of apostle. It seems, because Paul is going to address the subject of financial burden later in this passage (1 Thess. 2:9), this phrase was to combine the thoughts of support and esteem. Findley and Moffatt both hold this view. Therefore, this phrase captures the thought of covetousness, seeking the glory of men and motive of self-interest.

The word "apostles" has the force of the word "missionaries", which is the corresponding term from the Latin. It can be used in a technical or nontechnical sense. The technical sense would refer to Paul alone. In light of the plural, which is used throughout this passage ("our heart" 1 Thess. 2:4; "our own lives" 1Thess 2:8), it is unnecessary to interpret *apostle* in its technical sense.

Leaders should not use their position to obtain what

they want, nor should they use their position as an opportunity to climb the ladder to a higher position, with yet more authority. If throughout the leader's leadership life, they are given more and more responsibility, they should be humbled at the opportunity and not be arrogant or prideful. "…Yes, all of *you* be submissive to one another and be clothed with humility, for

> *'God resists the proud,*
> *But gives grace to the humble'."*
> *1Pet. 5:5*

It will help the leader to be humble if they realize others are necessary to accomplish their leadership goals. The leader cannot do it alone. A Shona proverb states, "One finger does not crush ice."[60] "Therefore, humble yourselves under the mighty hand of God, that He may exalt you in due time." 1 Pet. 5:5,6).

Now, in chapter three, Paul will leave the fleshly motives that need to be omitted in the biblical leader's life to develop godly motives that should to be included.

[28] "παράκλησις": this noun basically means "a calling to one's side". However, it is used with a wide variety of meanings according to the circumstances of those to whom it is directed. Fee, on page 59, footnote 25, states this word is a term which implies an appeal to the hearers' emotions as well as to their intellect. "For our exhortation" Paul here uses παράκλησις,to speak in broad terms about his preaching of the gospel, in which he urges or appeals to people to respond to God's salvation (cf. the verb form παρακαλοῦντος in 2 Cor 5:20). *The NET Bible*' p. w

[29] "πλάνης": a *wandering; deceit, deception, delusion, imposture, fraud,* Mt. 27:64; 1 Thess. 2:3; *seduction, deceiving,* Eph. 4:14; 2 Thess. 2:11; 1 Jn. 4:6; *error, false opinion,* 2 Pet. 3:17; *wandering* from the path of truth and virtue, *perverseness, wickedness, sin,* Rom. 1:27; Jas. 5:20; 2 Pet. 2:18; Jude 11. *Mounce Concise Greek-English Dictionary of the New Testament,* Accordance Bible Software electronic ed. 12.3.0 (2011).

[30] "ἀκαθαρσίας": this noun when defined outside of its context usually means *uncleanness; lewdness* and sometimes in context can mean *impure motives. Mounce Greek-English Dictionary of the New Testament,* Accordance electronic ed. 12.3.0. (2011).

[31] "δολιόω", "δόλος", ου,m: to deceive by using trickery and falsehood - 'to deceive, to trick into, treachery. δολιόω : ταῖς γλώσσαις αὐτων ἐδολιοῦσαν 'with their tongues they keep deceiving' Rom. 3:13. δόλος: συνεβουλεύσαντο ἵνα τὸν Ἰησοῦν δόλῳ κρατήσωσιν 'they made plans to arrest Jesus by means of treachery' Mt. 26:4. Johannes P. Louw & Eugene A. Nida *Greek-English Lexicon of the New Testament Based on Semantic,* Accordance electronic ed. 12.3.0 (New York: United Bible Societies, 2011).

[32] J.B. Lightfoot, *Notes on the Epistles of St. Paul.* Reprint. (Grand Rapids: Zondervan, 1957), 20-21.

[33] George G. Findlay, "The Epistles of Paul the Apostle to the Thessalonians" in *The Cambridge Greek Testament.* (Cambridge: U. Press, 1904), 37.

[34] Glenn L. Green, *The Letters to the Thessalonians* (Grand Rapids: William Eerdmans Publishing Company, 2002), 119.

[35] "δοκιμάζω"; "δοκιμή", ῆς f; "δοκίμιον", ου n; "δοκιμασία", ας f: to try to learn the genuineness of something by examination and testing, often through actual use - 'to test, to examine, to try to determine the genuineness of, testing to approve.' Johannes

P. Louw & Eugene A. Nida, *Greek-English Lexicon of the New Testament Based on Semanti*. Accordance electronic ed. 12.3.0 (New York: United Bible Societies, 2011). The Greek form in this verse is perfect, middle, indicative, 1ˢᵗ person plural.

[36] Cleon, L. Rogers Jr., & Cleon, L. Rogers III, *The New Linguistic and Exegetical Key to the Greek New Testament*. (Grand Rapids: Zondervan Publishing House, 1998), 473.

[37] The reader should consult the following resources: *Lordship Salvation*, Charles C. Bing (Grace Life); *Absolutely Free*, Zane C. Hodges (Zondervan Publishing House and Redencion Viva); *So Great Salvation*, Charles C. Ryrie (Victor Books).

[38] J.B. Hixson, Rick Whitmire, Roy B. Zuck, eds., *Freely By His Grace: Classical Free Grace Theology* (Duluth: Grace Gospel Press, 2012), 37.

[39] Glenn L. Green, *The Letters to the Thessalonians*, 121.

[40] "*κολακεία*": the word contains the idea of deception for selfish ends. It is flattery not merely for the sake of giving pleasure to others but for the sake of self-interest. (Linguistic and Exegetical Key to the Greek New Testament p. 473 [LEK]).

[41] "*ἐγενήθημεν*": aorist, indicative, passive (dep.) *γίνομαι*. With the flexibility of this Greek verb, whose basic meaning is "come to be", it here can mean something like, "we were among you" hence "lived among you". The NKJV interestingly abandoned its "literal" posture here and rendered it "used", thus putting the emphasis (correctly) on the prepositional phrases alone. (Fee: 62, footnote).

[42] "*πλεονεξία*": a strong desire to acquire more and more material possessions or [p. 292] to possess more things than other people have, all irrespective of need — 'greed, avarice, covetousness.' Johannes P. Louw & Eugene A. Nida, *Greek-English Lexicon of the New Testament Based on Semanti*. Accordance electronic ed. 12.3.0 (New York: United Bible Societies, 2011).

[43] Frame, *First and Second Thessalonians: The International Critical Commen-tary*, 97-98.

[44] Henry Bettenson, "The Didache" *Documents of the Christian Church* (London: Oxford University Press, 1963), 91-92.

[45] G.K. Beale, *1-2 Thessalonians* (Downers Grove: IVP Academic, 2003), 71.

[46] Green, *The Letters to the Thessalonians*, 122-123.

[47] "*ζητέω:*" to attempt to attain some state or condition — 'to attempt to find, to try to [p. 152] be.' *καὶ ἀπὸ τότε ἐζήτει*

εὐκαιρίαν ἵνα αὐτὸν παραδῷ and from then on he attempted to find favorable circumstances in order to betray him' Mt 26:16. (*Louw and Nida*, Accordance Bible Software). In this context, οὔτε ζηοῦντες is a present participle with the negative οὔτε which denies any practice or habit of seeking "glory of Men".

[48] "δόξα": radiance, glory, repute; δοξάζω: praise, glorify; ἔνδοξος honoured, glorious; ἐνδοξάζω / ἐνδοξάζομαι: honour, glorify; συνδοξάζω: glorify together; κενόδοξος: desirous of praise, conceited, boastful; κενοδοξία: desire for praise, conceit, vanity, illusion. *New International Dictionary of the NewTestament*, Accordance electornic ed. 12.3.0. (Grand Rapids: Zondervan Publishing House, 1986).

[49] Green, *The Letters to the Thessalonians,*123.

[50] D. Edmond Hiebert, *The Thessalonian Epistles* (Chicago: Moody Press, 1971). pp. 90-91.

[51] Green, *The Letters to the Thessalonians,* 124.

[52] C.F. Hogg and W.E. Vine, *The Epistles to the Thessalonians*. (Fincastle: Scripture Truth Book Company, 1959), 58.

[53] Robert N. Wilkins ed., *The Grace New Testament Commentary*. (Denton: Grace Evangelical Society, 2010), 934.

[54] Frame, *First and Second Thessalonians: The International Critical Commen-tary,* 99.

[55] Dio Chrysoston 32:11; 12:5; 8:33; 77/78:27. Cited in Green, *The Letters to the Thessalonians,*124.

[56] δύναμαι; δυνατέω (derivatives of δύναμις 'ability,'): to be able to do or to experience something — 'can, to be able to.' Johannes P. Louw & Eugene A. Nida, *Greek-English Lexicon of the New Testament Based on Semanti*. Accordance electronic ed. 12.3.0 (New York: United Bible Societies, 2011).

[57] Βάρει ἐιμί (an idiom, literally 'to be in weight'; see 86.1): to insist on one's importance or worth — 'to insist on one's worth, to claim one's importance.' δυνάμενοι ἐν βάρει εἶναι 'we could have insisted on our importance' 1Th. 2:6b.

[58] ἀπόστολος (derivative of ἀποστέλλω 'to send a message,'): one who is sent with a message — 'messenger.' οὐδέ ἀπόστολος μείζων τοῦ πέμψαντος αὐτόν no messenger is greater than the one who sent him' John 13:16.

[59] Findlay, "Thessalonians" *Cambridge Greek Testament*, 66.

[60] John Jusu, Supervising Editor, *Africa Study Bible*, 1649.

CHAPTER 3

THE MODEL OF A LEADER

1 THESSALONIANS 2:7-12
(CHARACTERISTICS TO BE INCLUDE)

1 Thessalonians 2:7

"But we were gentle among you, just as a nursing mother cherishes her own children."

"ἀλλ᾽ ἐγενήθημεν ἤπιοι⁶¹ ἐν μέσῳ ὑμῶν ὡς ἄν τροφὸς ⁶² θάλπη⁶³ τὰ ἑαυτῆς τέκνα,"

The conjunction "but" (ἀλλὰ) again introduces the positive side of the leader's conduct in contrast to the preceding negative attributes. In this verse, Paul discusses a characteristic of the leader that is a personal skill - engaging individuals. Being the leader is more than just preaching and teaching, important as that is. One of the downfalls of a megachurch is that many times the leaders have little ministry to individuals in the congregation outside of group encounters. Therefore, as a church grows people must learn to minister to one another.

To launch this kind of ministry, leaders and groups need to study and apply the "one another's" of the New Testament, cf. Gene Getz *One Another Series*. Paul in Ephesians 4:11,12 states one of the major responsibilities of the leaders of any ministry, "…He Himself gave some *to be* apostles, some prophets, some evangelists, and some pastors and teachers, *for the equipping of the saints for the work of ministry, for the edifying of the body of Christ…*" (italics mine). This is more than just showing up on Sunday for a 30-minute sermon. Rather, it means interacting with individuals with the goal of developing the following attributes.

The first positive attribute of the leader is to be "gentle". This has the idea of showing kindness.[64] Paul and his missionary team avoided any harsh and high-handed assumption of authority. "All was tenderness and devotion, fostering and protecting care in their relations to those Thessalonian Christians who had won their hearts."[65] The words "among you" point to the leader as the center of a group. This demonstrated, as they were teaching, they were also building a relationship with the believers. They held the position of gentle teachers surrounded by their students. "Far from ascending a lofty pinnacle and speaking down to their followers, the missionaries freely mingled with them".[66]

After asserting his concern for gentleness, Paul follows with a figurative statement, "...just as a nursing mother cherishes her own children". When the Thessalonians accepted the gospel they, like children, were in need of gentle kindness that the leaders provided. Paul uses an example of a "wet nurse". This nurse ("nursing mother" NKJV) was usually a woman who was hired to nurse and care for the child of another person. The word "cherishes" properly means "to warm";

it was used of birds covering their young with their feathers to warm and protect them (Deut. 22:6 LXX). "The nurse was in charge of feeding the child, but her job also included caring for and even educating the infant."[67] This picture shows the unselfish conduct of the missionaries in dealing with their converts. Leaders must care for their converts with no thought of honor and glory for themselves. Some commentators believe the word "her own children" suggest that this nurse was apparently the mother herself.[68] However, the word "nourisher" ($\tau\rho o\phi\grave{o}\varsigma$) does not usually refer to the birth mother.

Therefore, the leader must remember it is not easy to be a "nourisher". Even Moses felt the burden of caring for God's people. "Was it I who conceived all these people? Was it I who brought them forth, that Thou shouldest say to me, 'Carry them in your bosom as a nurse carries a nursing infant, to the land which Thou didst swear to their fathers'?" (Num. 11:12 NASB). "But if we do not nurse the new Christians on the milk of the

44

Word, they can never mature to appreciate the meat of the Word."[69] The writer of Hebrews declares,

> "Being designated by God as a high priest according to the order of Melchizedek. Concerning him, we have much to say, and *it is* hard to explain, since you have become dull of hearing. For though by this time you ought to be teachers, you have need again for someone to teach you the elementary principles of the oracles of God, and you have come to need milk and not solid food. For everyone who partakes *only* of milk is not accustomed to the word of righteousness, for he is a babe. But solid food is for the mature, who because of practice have their senses trained to discern good and evil" (Heb. 5:10-14).

Additionally, the leader must remember growing believers can try their patience. "In Liberia there is a common proverb that says, 'There is no dumpsite for a spoiled child'. Other West African cultures say, 'There is no bush to throw a bad child'."[70] This proverb demonstrates it is a priority for the leader to be gentle and patient with babes in Christ.

1 Thessalonians 2:8a

"So, affectionately longing for you..."

"Οὕτως[71] ὁμειρόμενοι[72] ὑμῶν..."

It goes without saying that Paul and his missionary team had a real love/affection for the believers in Thessalonica. If the leader is going to lead individuals from justification to sanctification and on to glorification, it is going to take sacrificial love. It is one thing to lead someone to the Savior, it is quite another thing to guide them in their spiritual development. Discipling an individual may be the most difficult ministry for the leader. This is seen in the megachurch model in North America and in the evangelistic model in the majority world. Many times, both the megachurch and evangelistic models have grown so rapidly that even if discipleship is desired there are not enough mature believers, nor the resources, to keep abreast of the growth. In the evangelistic model of the majority world, the church has grown over a long period of time. However, discipleship was not the emphasis and churches ended up with a large "denomination" where members usually have an acceptable biblical knowledge but are lacking in spiritual maturity. It is one thing to be a hearer of the word and another thing to be a doer of the word (James 1:22-25). This would be corrected if the leader put emphasis on quality, i.e. spiritual maturity, allowing the church to grow numerically because the believers are growing spiritually, thus fulfilling the great commission by spiritual reproduction (evangelism and discipleship).

1 Thessalonians 2:8b

"…we were well pleased to impart to you not only the gospel of God, but also our own lives, because you had become dear to us."

"…εὐδοκοῦμεν[73] μεταδοῦναι[74] ὑμῖν οὐ μόνον τὸ εὐαγγέλιον τοῦ θεοῦ, ἀλλὰ καὶ Τὰς ἑαυτῶν ψυχὰ ς[75], διότι ἀγαπητοὶ[76] ἡμῖν γεγένησθε."

"We were well pleased" indicates the missionaries were making a free choice. They were not driven by guilt or impure motives but they were sharing the gospel and their lives because these missionaries loved these believers. In the Western world, we have so distorted love into nothing more than a sensual act. As Jesus portrayed in the New Testament, love is so much more. When ones go to the tomb of Lazarus in John chapter eleven, Jesus was weeping because His friend had died. However, the reaction of the Jews standing nearby is revealing, "Then the Jews said, *'See how He loved him!'*" (italics mine) (John 11:36). It was Jesus who declared what the two greatest commandments are, "And you shall love the LORD your God with all your heart, with all your soul, with all your mind, and with all your strength. This *is* the first commandment. And the second, like *it, is* this: You shall love your neighbor as yourself. There is no other commandment greater than these" (Mark 12:30,31). Scot McKnight has called this the Jesus Creed.[77]

I remember as a young missionary in Ethiopia going to our language school instructor and revealing to her that I did not love Ethiopians, I did not even like them! I asked her, "What should I do?" She was a very wise missionary and directed my attention to 2 Cor. 5:14, "For the love of Christ compels us…". She reminded me that Christ loved me when I was unlovable and that same love that Christ had for me compels me to love the people that God had called me to serve. I'm glad to report that I fell in love with the people of Ethiopia and the country. As leaders, more must be done than just loving the gospel of our Lord and Savior Jesus Christ. Leaders must love sacrificially those they lead. Much of ministry is more caught than taught.

1 Thessalonians 2:9

"For you remember, brethren, our labor and toil; for laboring night and day, that we might not be a burden to any of you, we preached to you the gospel of God."

"Μνημονεύετε⁷⁸ γάρ,ἀδελφοί τὸν κόπον ἡμῶν καὶ τὸν μόχθον νυκτὸς⁷⁹ καὶ ἡμέρας ἐργαζόμενοι⁸⁰ πρὸς τὸ μὴ ἐπιβαρῆσαι⁸¹ τινα ὑμῶν ἐκηρύξαμεν⁸² εἰς ὑμᾶς τὸ εὐαγγέλιον τοῦ θεοῦ."

For you remember, brethren…", "brethren" is a term that speaks of a close and intimate relationship like that between members of a family (1 Cor. 4:14,17; Eph. 5:1; Phi. 2:12; 4:1; Phil. 16). Paul and his missionary team were simply asking the Thessalonians to remember the missionaries' ministry among them. What are some of things they should recall?

Fee's comments are instructive at this point:

> Although we can never know for certain, it seems altogether likely that when Paul, Silas, and Timothy came to Thessalonica, they sensed the need not to live off the largesse of these new believers. Indeed, he expresses the need in terms of concern for them: 'in order not to be a burden to any of you.' And while not stated as such, the whole passage (1Thess. 2:1-12) indicates that Paul had been led by the Spirit in that decision, since otherwise their accepting free "room and board" could have been used against them. Now, at the end of the present argument, Paul reminds the Thessalonians themselves of this reality-with emphasis on the toilsome nature of his everyday work that had freed him up to 'preached to you the gospel of God'.[83]

Therefore, these believers remembered how Paul and his missionary team had ministered among them. This verse demonstrates that ministry is not for the faint of heart. These words "labor and toil" are words that mean this missionary team gave everything they could to the preaching of the gospel and the giving of their lives to believers in Thessalonica! In fact, not only is this seen in these two words, but Paul also emphasizes their work ethic by the phrase "...laboring night and day" which is better translated "during the night as well as the day". This text is not asking leaders to abandon their families, rather, it is stating there is no place for laziness in ministry. Ministry is not a 40 hour a week job. Paul is simply saying servants of the Lord need to give more to their ministry than just the task of preaching the gospel, as important as that is. These servants must of necessity give of themselves to the ministry that God has called them. Paul structures the last part of the verse using a purpose clause, "...for the purpose of not becoming a burden to any of you..." (literal translation of 1Thess. 2:9b). One of the reasons that Paul and his missionary team worked so hard was not be a burden to the church. This does not mean that the leader is not worthy of wages, "…The laborer *is* worthy of his wages". (1 Tim. 5:18b). But this does not mean to the extent of causing a financial burden to the converts that would indicate greed behind the leader's preaching. Even the Mishnah instructed teachers of the Torah not to make gain from their teaching. "Thus you have learned: Whoever derives worldly benefit from teachings of Torah takes his life from the world."[84]

Having said all of this, it is necessary for the church in the West and in the majority world to address this issue. I have been in many classes in Ethiopia where dedicated missionary leaders have brought up the issue of insufficient wages for them to take care of their families. The church cannot hide under the phrase "live by faith" when the Bible clearly states that we need to pay leaders/missionaries adequately because they are worthy of their wages! Maybe it would be better to send out fewer missionaries and take care of the ones already commissioned, or it may be that the church needs to make the great commission its top priority.

1 Thessalonians 2:10

"You *are* witnesses, and God *also,* how devoutly and justly and blamelessly we behaved ourselves among you who believe;"

"Ὑμεῖς μάρτυρες καὶ ὁ θεός ὡς ὁσίως[85] καὶ δικαίως[86] καὶ ἀμέμπτως[87] ὑμῖν τοῖς πιστεύουσιν[88] ἐγενήθημεν."[89]

Paul reminds the Thessalonians that they were witnesses of his missionary team's conduct. Having seen the character of these servants of God, they could testify to their behavior. Paul knows that only God can see the genuineness of a servant's motive (1 Thess. 2:4) but, that being said, their ministry is subject to both human and divine observation. So, what did the Thessalonians observe in those who were ministering among them? What they observed is seen in a series of adverbs. The first adverb is the word translated "devoutly". This Greek word is related to the ordinary word rendered "holy" (ἅγιος) in the New Testament. It basically means "holy manner" but is usually translated "holy" (NET,

ESV, NIV-2011) or "devoutly" (NKJV, NASB, NCSB). This word "points to the inner disposition which gives regard to the sanctities of life".[90] Fee believes this "word emphasizes living in a way that is pleasing God, thus picking up on God as his witness".[91] Again, Paul might be addressing the pure motives which the believers possessed when his missionary team ministered among them. It cannot be emphasized enough - leaders work from the inside out. It is more about "being" than "doing". Therefore, the leader must be asking God to develop their inner life toward Christlikeness. "But we all, with unveiled face, beholding as in a mirror the glory of the Lord, *are being transformed* into the same image from glory to glory, just as by the Spirit of the Lord" (2 Cor. 3:18) (italics mine). The verb "are being transformed" ($\mu\epsilon\tau\alpha\mu\rho\rho\phi\omega\nu\mu\epsilon\theta\alpha$) is a present passive meaning that the Holy Spirit is involved in the process of metamorphosis - change from the inside out - beginning with the new birth (John 3:3,5) and continuing by sanctification throughout life (John 17:17). The leader must remember they need to surrender to the Spirit of God as He does the work of sanctification.

The next adverb that Paul uses is "justly", demonstrating what the Thessalonians should have witnessed in the lives of Paul and his missionary team. This word reveals the kind of "...conduct that comes up to full standard of what is right or just and thus relates to the performance of the duties of life".[92] The word "justly" covers the moral aspect of the leader. Therefore, integrity and upright conduct must always be the mark of biblical leadership. Over against these two positive words of character, Paul uses the negative adverb "blamelessly", literally "unblamably". "This word claims an irreproachable conduct as a whole, indicating that no charges can be maintained, whatever charges might be made against them"[93] The leader cannot keep individuals from bringing false charges against them, however, it is God who knows the heart. The leader needs to be sure that their motives are pure and their heart is right before God. Should the leader try to defend themselves? Yes, if possible, but most of the time it will be next to impossible. The leader must not be obsessed with defending themselves because, if they do, it will so distract them that their ministry could be destroyed. It is best right from the beginning for the leader to keep themselves from every appearance of evil. "Abstain from every form of evil." (1 Thess. 5:22). First and foremost, this missionary team believed their responsibility was to the believers in Thessalonica, "we behaved ourselves among you who believe" (1 Thess. 2:10b).

1 Thessalonians 2:11,12

"as you know how we exhorted, and comforted, and charged every one of you, as a father *does* his own children, that you would walk worthy of God who calls you into His own kingdom and glory."

"καθάπερ οἴδατε[94], ὡς ἕνα ἕκαστον ὑμῶν ὡς πατὴρ τέκνα ἑαυτοῦ[95] παρακαλοῦντες[96] ὑμᾶς καὶ παραμυθούμενοι[97] καὶ μαρτυρόμενοι[98] εἰς τὸ περιπατεῖν[99] ὑμᾶς ἀξίως[100] τοῦ θεοῦ τοῦ καλοῦ ντος ὑμᾶς εἰς τὴν ἑαυτοῦ βασιλείαν καὶ δόξαν."

Paul, having used the example of a "nursing mother" (1Thess. 2:7), now changes his illustration to that of a father. Paul and his missionary team see these believers as their children (τέκνα ἑαυτου) This indicates that these missionaries were devoted to the task of training and instruction. They lived such virtuous lives before the believers at Thessalonica that Paul could say, "as you know". What a great testimony these missionaries demonstrated before this newly planted church. It is so important for the leader to live a holy life before others. This is characterized in other Pauline Epistles as "walking in the Spirit" and being "led by the Spirit" (Gal. 5:16-26). The leadership characteristics that follow reveal that these leaders were filled with the Holy Spirit; what they were on the inside is like a fountain flowing into their ministry to this young church. Lünemann writes, "For if anyone can be truly desirous that others walk virtuously, this presupposed the endeavor after virtue in himself."[101]

In 1Thess. 2:11, the three participles that Paul uses are in the present tense which points to the activities as their continual practice. Paul begins by reminding the believers that they "exhorted" them. Although this word can be translated "exhort" (NKJV), in this context it is better translated "appeal" (NEB) (cf. footnote 96). This word denotes a strong appeal for these believers to have lives that would be worthy of their calling. This is anything but a suggestion. It is necessary to build strong relationships with the believers. The leader must be very careful that their relationships are of such a nature that they can still give "strong appeals" to live godly lives. It will be necessary when discipling new believers to challenge them directly. This is part of being a courageous leader. It is good to remember what God said to Joshua as he was about to lead the children of Israel into the land of Canaan: "Have I not commanded you? Be strong and of good courage; do not be afraid, nor be dismayed, for the LORD your God *is* with you wherever you go" (Josh. 1:9).

Paul's second present participle is to remind the believers that, when he and his missionary team were in Thessalonica, they continually "comforted" them. This is a soft word that might be translated care-fronting. Sometimes this word is translated "console". There is a place for strong exhortation but there is also a place for listening, not talking, and just allowing the disciple to unburden their heart. Sometimes the leader can be so concerned with what they have to teach that they forget the disciple may have concerns and questions they have a desire to ask. This word "comforted" describes the kind of environment that is needed for discipling. If the leader has this kind of attitude, they are able to build people up especially in times of difficulty, all of which points to the apostle's examples of mothers (1Thess. 2:7) and fathers (1Thess. 2:11), the imagery in this passage.

Paul's third participle in this sentence is the continual "charging" of his fellow believers. This word basically means "to invoke witnesses", "to declare solemnly" or "to insist". But what was Paul charging them to do? Paul answers this question in 1Thess. 2:12. First, consider that all three of these participles carry with them the spirit of fatherhood. These words reveal the passion that Paul so often portrayed toward those he led. It is necessary for the leader to have this kind of passion portrayed in these three words when they are leading, especially new believers!

1Thess. 2:12 gives substance to these three participles. This verse begins in the Greek with a purpose construction, "in order that" (lit.). Paul was imploring them to "walk worthy of God". "Walk" has the idea of "going back and forth", equaling "living", or "behaving" in a certain manner. In this context, Paul was challenging the believers to live lives pleasing to God who has summonsed, "called", them in the first place. All Christians have been given a royal summons by God Himself, inviting them to the glorious privilege of co-reigning with Christ in the life to come (2 Tim. 2:12; Rev. 2:26-27; 3:21). But not all Christians will be chosen to co-reign (Rom. 8:17b; 2 Tim. 2:12). The qualifier for co-reigning is living a life worthy of God who is calling us into His kingdom and glory. Paul uses a different metaphor in 1 Cor. 3:11-15. In that passage, a Christian's life is seen as the building of a house with different types of material. The materials, gold, silver and precious stones, depict a life lived worthy of God.

Paul's reference to the kingdom in 1 Thess. 2:12 refers to the millennial kingdom where Christ will reign as King of Kings and Lord of Lords (Rev. 20:1-6). At the end of His 1000 reign, He will deliver up His kingdom to His Father and the eternal kingdom will be forever and forever. "Then *comes* the end, when He delivers the kingdom to God the Father, when He puts an end to all rule and all authority and power" (1 Cor. 15:24).

In conclusion, G.K. Beale has an excellent summary of these twelve verses:

> "The main point of 2:1-12 is that Paul's witness among the Thessalonians was effective (1Thess. 2:1) because it was based on his bold proclamation of the truth of the gospel (1Thess. 2:2). The two motives undergirding and inspiring this testimony were that Paul wanted to please God (1Thess. 2:3-4) and wanted others to please God in order to glorify him (1Thess. 2:5-12). That the first motive is stated before the second is significant: one must want to please God

before one can truly desire others to want to please God. The kind of attitudes and lifestyle that Paul depicts in 1Thess. 2:2-12 were pleasing to God and resulted in influencing others for the gospel because the life he lived was inextricably linked to the truth he preached. When we do not live in a manner that demonstrates the truth of the good news, we do not please God and do not have a godly boldness. Rather, what we say about the gospel with our lips may have no lasting persuasion and effectiveness for the lives of the hearers, with the result that they will not please God and inherit his glorious kingdom."[102]

---

[61] "ἐγενήθημεν ἤπιοι": (we were gentle) a text-critical issue confronts us here. While some ancient manuscripts read "gentle" (ἤπιοι), others insert a word that differs by only one Greek letter making the word, "infants" (νήπιοι). The evidence from the manuscripts themselves favors the reading "infants," but many commentators and translators prefer the reading "gentle," since it makes what appears to be a better sense of the verse. How could we understand the logic of the argument if the apostles claimed to be "infants" among the Thessalonians and then compare that state with maternal care: "like a mother cherishes for her own children?" (Green: p.127).

[62] "τροφὸς": a person who functions as a substitute for a mother in the process of rearing children — nursemaid, nurse (in the British, not American, sense). ἐγενήθημεν νήπιοι ἐν μέσῳ ὑμῶν ὡς ἐάν τροφὸς θάλπῃ τὰ ἑαυτῆς τέκνα, "we were as gentle with you as a nurse caring for her children" 1Thess. 2:7. It is possible that in 1Thess. 2:7 τροφός may mean a mother nursing and rearing her children. Johannes P. Louw & Eugene A. Nida, *Greek-English Lexicon of the New Testament Based on*

Semanti. Accordance electronic ed. 12.3.0 (New York: United Bible Societies, 2011).

[63] "θάλπη": Active, Subjective 3ʳᵈ, Singular θάλπω: to take care of, with the implication of cherishing and concern for — 'to take care of.' Οὐδεὶς γὰρ ποτε τὴν ἑαυτοῦ σάρκα ἐμίσησεν ἀλλὰ ἐκτρέφει καὶ θάλπει αὐτήν "no one ever hates his own body; instead, he feeds it and takes care of it" Eph. 5:29. It may be useful in some instances to translate "and takes care of it" in Eph. 5:29, as "'and gives to his own body whatever is needed' or 'and does for himself whatever is necessary'".

[64] "ἤπιος" α,ον: pertaining to being gentle, with the implication of kindness — "gentle, kind".

[65] James Moffatt, "First and Second Epistles of Paul the Apostle to Thessalonians" *The Expositor's Greek New Testament.* Vol. 4 ed. W. Robertson Nicoll (Grand Rapids: Wm. B. Eerdmans Publishing Company, 2002), 27.

[66] Hiebert, *The Thessalonian Epistles,* 95.

[67] Green, *The Letters to the Thessalonians,*129.

[68] Hiebert, *The Thessalonian Epistle,* 95.

[69] Warren W. Wiersbe, *The Wiersbe Bible Commentary, New Testament.* (Colorado Springs: David C. Cook, 2007), 709.

[70] John Jusu, Supervising Editor, *Africa Study Bible,* 1261.

[71] "Οὕτως": "So" "'thus, in this manner' resumes the thought of the missionaries' conduct expressed in 1Thess. 2:7 but reemphasizes it by dropping the figure and stating the literal manner in which their conduct found expression" (Hiebert: 95).

[72] "ὁμειρόμενοι": present, middle (dep.), participle, ὁμείρομαι (to have kindly feeling for). The meaning of this rare word is not wholly clear, but it obviously expresses intensity of feeling. Paul used this word in 1 Thess. 2:8 to show that he does not serve the church merely in obedience to his commission but out of heartfelt love for it. *New International Dictionary of the New Testament,* Accordance electronic ed. 12.3.0. (Grand Rapids: Zondervan Publishing House, 1986). "It is used on a grave inscription describing the parents' sad yearning for their dead child and seems to indicate deep affection and great attraction (James Hope Moulton and George Moulton, *The Vocabulary of the Greek New Testament* (London: Hodder & Stoughton, 1952). p.22). "This is also a word of endearment derived from the language of the nursery." (Moulton, p.22)

Dan A. Esteline, Sr.

[73] "*εὐδοκοῦμεν*": imperfect, active, indicative, 1st person, plural, *εὐδοκέω*. "This is a verb whose primary meaning is 'to take pleasure in something,' but which in some contexts can also mean 'to resolve' or 'to consent'." (Fee: p.75). The imperfect tense testified that with continued hearty good will they acted.

[74] "*μεταδοῦναι*": aorist, active, infinitive, *μεταδίδωμι*. The preposition *μετα* prefixed to the infinitive brings out the thought that the missionaries did not merely give a gift but rather imparted something which they desired to share with Thessalonians.

[75] "*ψυχὰς*", "*ψυχη*": this denotes their inner being, the climax of their giving. This word also denotes their inner being, their personality.

[76] "*ἀγαπητοί*", "*ἀγαπητός*" pertaining to one who or that which is loved — "object of one's affection, one who is loved, beloved, dear" Johannes P. Louw & Eugene A. Nida, *Greek-English Lexicon of the New Testament Based on Semanti.* Accordance electronic ed. 12.3.0 (New York: United Bible Societies, 2011).

[77] Scot McKnight, *The Jesus Creed.* (Brewster Massachuetts: Paraclete Press, 2004), 4.

[78] "*μνημονεύετε*", present, active, imperative, 2nd plural *μνημονεύω,μιμνήσκομαι, ηνήμη,ης f: μνεία,ας f:* to recall information from memory, but without necessarily the implication that persons have actually forgotten — "to remember, to recall, to think about again, memory, remembrance". Johannes P. Louw & Eugene A. Nida, *Greek-English Lexicon of the New Testament Based on Semanti.* Accordance electronic ed. 12.3.0 (New York: United Bible Societies, 2011).

[79] "*τὸν κόπον ἡμῶν καὶ τὸν μόχθον νυκτὸς*": a genitive of time = "during the night as well as the day". *κόπον* "labor" indicates the weariness and fatigue arising from continued strenuous activity, *μόχθον* "toil" points to the outward difficulties that must be overcome. (Hiebert: p.97).

[80] "*ἐργαζόμενοι*": present, middle (Dep.) participle *ἐργάζομαι.* This is the general word for "work" and it may be Paul's way of combining in one word the idea of labor and toil.

[81] "*πρὸς τὸ μὴ ἐπιβαρῆσαι*": this is one of the common ways to introduce the idea of purpose, *πρὸς το* plus the infinitive *ἐπιβαρῆσαι. ἐπιβαρῆσαι /ἐπιβαρέω* means to place a weight on someone, to be burdensome, to make demands. (Rogers: p.474).

[82] "ἐκηρύξαμεν": aorist, active, indicative, first person, plural, κηρύσσω. This means to announce in a formal or official manner by means of a herald or one who functions as a herald — "to announce, to proclaim".

[83] Gordon D. Fee, *The First and Second Letters to the Thessalonians*. (GrandRapids: William B. Eerdmans Publishing Company, 2009), 78.

[84] Translated by J. Neusner, *The Mishnah: A New Translation* (New Haven: Yale University Press, 1988), 675. (*Aboth 4:5*).

[85] "ὁσίως" Adverb, "ὅσιος", α, ον: pertaining to being dedicated or consecrated to the service of God — "devout, godly, dedicated." Johannes P. Louw & Eugene A. Nida, *Greek-English Lexicon of the New Testament Based on Semanti*. Accordance electronic ed. 12.3.0 (New York: United Bible Societies, 2011).

[86] "δικαίως": denotes the kind of conduct that comes up to the full standard of what is right or just and thus relates to the performance of the duties of life. (Hiebert: p.101).

[87] "ἀμέμπτως": "It claims an irreproachable conduct as a whole, indicating that no charges can be maintained, whatever charges might be made against them." (Hiebert: p. 102) "It affixes the seal of approval both by God and man." (Findlay: p.70).

[88] "πιστεύουσιν:" present, active, participle, masculine, plural, dative, πιστεύω. The appositional articular participle pictures them as characterized by their continuing faith.

[89] "ἐγενήθημεν": aorist, passive, indicative, first person, plural γίνομαι.

[90] Hiebert, *The Thessalonian Epistles*, 101.

[91] Fee, *The First and Second Letters to the Thessalonians*, 79.

[92] Hiebert, *The Thessalonian Epistles*, 101.

[93] Ibid., 102.

[94] "καθάπερ οἴδατε", "as you know" is a strong comparative particle καθάπερ. The first part of the words marks the comparison and the last part is the latitude of the application. It introduces a confirmatory appeal to the individual hearers. (Rogers: p. 474).

[95] This is a structurally defective sentence because of the lack of a finite verb. Rather than adding words like "dealt with" (ASV) or "does" (NKJV), it seems better to resume the finite verb ἐγενήθημεν,"you are", from verse 10 to form a paraphrastic construction with the participles.

Dan A. Esteline, Sr.

[96] "παρακαλοῦντες", present, active, participle παρακαλέω. This word comes from two Greek words καλέω, "to call", παρα, "alongside of'". It is a general word used for exhorting that indicates a strong appeal made for someone to adopt a suitable course of action. Findlay calls the verb "the general term for animating address." (Findlay: p. 47).

[97] "παραμυθούμενοι": present, middle (dep), participle παραμυθέομαι is made from παρα, "toward", and μυθέομαι, "to speak", παραμυθέομαι basic sense "to speak to someone in a friendly way". With reference to what ought to be done, it develops the sense "to admonish," with reference to what has been done, the sense "to console". *New International Dictionary of the New Testament*, Accordance electronic ed. 12.3.0. (Grand Rapids: Zondervan Publishing House, 1986). This word denotes the soothing and encouraging side of exhortation, inspiring someone to continue the desired course of action.

[98] "μαρτυρόμενοι": present, middle (dep), participle μαρτυρέω. This participle points to the solemnity and earnestness with which the appeal is made. This word comes from a verb which basically means "to invoke witnesses", hence "to declare solemnly, to insist". (Hiebert: p. 104).

[99] "περιπατεῖν": present, active, infinitive περιπατέω. Is a common word usually used as a figure of speech to denote moral conduct. It is also a compound word composed of the preposition περι, "around", and πατέω, "to walk", hence "to walk around to conduct one's self".

[100] "ἄξιος α,ον "ἀξίως": pertaining to being fitting or proper in corresponding to what should be expected — 'proper, properly, fitting, worthy of, correspond to.' Eph. 4:1. Johannes P. Louw & Eugene A. Nida, *Greek-English Lexicon of the New Testament Based on Semanti.* Accordance electronic ed. 12.3.0 (New York: United Bible Societies, 2011).

[101] Gottlieb Lünemann. "Critical and Exegetical Handbook of the Epistles of St. Paul to the Thessalonians." In *Meyer's Critical and Exegetical Commentary on the New Testament.* (Edinburgh: T. & T. Clark, 1884), 55.

[102] Beale, *1-2 Thessalonians*, 76.

APPENDICES

APPENDIX #1:
LEADERSHIP PRINCIPLES

The twenty-eight principles below are to be studied along with the exegetical commentary made above on each verse. Correct exegesis comes before application of these principles. <u>The leader will find blank pages (NOTEBOOK) at the end of this appendix to complete the exercises delineated in several of the principles</u>.

Application #1: Introduction

The background text for the ministry of Paul at Thessalonica is Acts 17:1-9. There are important ministry principles in this historical account of his ministry. These principles will be very helpful especially for the leader serving in the majority world.

- Principle #1: It appears that Paul had a strategic plan for reaching Thessalonica for Christ. The text states that he went to the synagogue "as his custom was". This indicates that Paul and his missionary team had a strategy for any Roman city that had a Jewish community. Being Jews themselves, attending the synagogue was a natural bridge for sharing the gospel. The leader needs to discover bridges that will give them opportunities to launch their ministry. This synagogue location gave Paul an opportunity to address individuals that were leaders among key people in the synagogue and perhaps in the city. Of course, strategic plans must always be seasoned with prayer seeking the wisdom of the Lord. **Read chapter 11, "Developing Vision and Strategy" (pp. 187-200), in *Leading Across Cultures* by James E. Plueddemann, cf. Mark 16:15 and Matthew 28:17-20. Using Plueddemann's model write an example of a strategic plan.**

- Principle #2: Paul's plan was not immediately accomplished. He stayed in Thessalonica at least three Sabbaths. This statement "three Sabbaths" (Acts 17:2) is probably an illustration of history compressed. There is ample evidence from 1 and 2 Thessalonians that a significant amount of time elapsed between Acts 17:4 and 5. These three missionaries had to have spent many months ministering to these new believers and winning others to Christ. Remember, just leading people to Christ is not a completion of the great commission. The leader will find the most difficult part of the great commission may well be the task of discipleship, it certainly takes more time. **What needs to be included in a discipleship curriculum?**

- Principle #3: First things first. Paul shared with the Thessalonians the death, resurrection and messiahship of Christ (Acts 17:3). The leader must not get sidetracked into other theological issues, e.g. creation. If they do, their engagement will end up in a fruitless argument that encourages no one to consider the claims of Christ. It is very important that the gospel be "explained and demonstrated" (Acts 17:3). Ingredients of the gospel are clear from this text: believing in the death, resurrection and messiahship of Christ. **Write a one page paper defining the gospel, include Scripture texts.**

- Principle #4: Understand the trichotomy of fear-power, shame-honor, and guilt-innocence culture paradigms. This is a technical subject of missiology and the leader should review the book *Honor and Shame: Unlocking the Door* by Roland Muller. Acts 17 explains which people were persuaded, both devout Greeks and leading women, but notes idolators were converted (1 Thess. 1:9). The word "joined" ($\pi\rho o\sigma\kappa\lambda\eta\rho\acute{o}\omega$) (Acts 17:4) could very well mean to follow as a disciple. Paul must have contextualized the gospel so they could understand it within their cultural paradigm. The leader's presentation of the gospel must be contextualized to be effective.

Read Part III, "Contextualizing Leadership" (pp.149-185), in *Leading Across Cultures* by James E. Plueddemann.

- Principle #5: Be prepared for persecution. Persecution is seldom fair or just. The unpersuaded Jews became envious, assembled evil men and set the city in an uproar. One of the reasons for persecution is exactly what the mob declared, "These who have turned the world upside down have come here too" (Acts 17:6b). Many times, the gospel from the world's perspective turns their world upside down. In any society, values, morals and ethics are destined to change. The danger of persecution is it usually flows over to the new believers and because of their immaturity may cause them to fall away (Matt. 13:20,21).

- Principle #6: God may intervene as He did with Jason and his household. The city officials took security from Jason and the others and then released them (Acts 17:9). It is necessary for the leader to trust God and allow Him to determine the outcome (Prov. 3:5,6; Matt. 28:20; 1 Pet. 5:7).

- Principle #7: Teach, teach and teach again. Even though Paul and his missionary team were at Thessalonica for a relatively short period of time they taught many subjects. The following subjects are alluded to in 1 Thessalonians: The Trinity (compare 1Thess. 1:1 with 1Thess. 1:5-6); the Holy Spirit (1Thess. 1:5-6; 4:8; 5:19); Christ's second advent (1Thess. 1:10; 2:19; 3:13; 4:14-17; 5:123); the Day of the Lord (1Thess. 5:1-3); assurance (1 Thess. 4:14-18); conversion (1Thess. 1:9); election (1Thess 1:4); resurrection (1Thess. 4:14-18); sanctification (1Thess. 4:3; 5:23); and Christian behavior (1Thess. 2:12; 4:1). **Write one page explaining what new believers should be taught.**

- Principle #8: Be sure the discipleship process is bearing fruit before the leader moves on to develop other leaders. In 1 Thess. 1:3 Paul observed three developing characteristics in this recently planted assembly of believers. He commended them for their "work of faith, labor of love, and patience of hope". These are indicators that these new believers were growing toward Christlikeness. **What spiritual fruit would you expect to see in a developing believer?**

- Principle #9: It is not cowardly to leave a ministry because the leader's life may be in danger. The believers sent Paul and Silas away by night to Berea (Acts 17:11). Of course, this decision must be done after prayer and fasting; but remember God had more ministries for Paul besides Thessalonica. This does not mean that the leader should always move. However, after seeking the Lord's wisdom, it is imperative to do what they believe is God's will.

Application #2: 1 Thessalonians 2:1,2

- Principle #10: Glory belongs to the Lord. "I *am* the LORD, that *is* My name; And My glory I will not give to another…" (Isa. 42:8). Who does not want a ministry to grow numerically? The truth is many times God places the leader in an area that is very difficult, e.g. the Jewish or Muslim world. But the leader's ministry and all ministry is in fact for God's glory. The leader must strive to give God the glory in everything that they do. In the final analysis, first and foremost a ministry is about HIM, not the leader! This does not mean that the leader will not develop the discipline that constitutes a ministry strategic plan. **Review chapter 1 in the main body of this paper.**

- Principle #11: Keep short accounts with God. Remember, the leader has feet of clay and that being true, they make mistakes - yes they sin! The leader needs to have a daily examination of their life and apply 1 John 1:9 in each and every sinful act. Remember, it is the leader's responsibility to confess their sin and it is God's responsibility to forgive and cleanse from all unrighteousness. An excellent outline to use for this examination time is the one by Lewis Sperry Chafer found in the main body of this paper on pages 13-14. **Do a thorough study of 1 John 1:9 and write one page on your observations.**

- Principle #12: There is no place for fear in the life of the leader - they must be courageous. Many individuals within the Christian community and outside that community believe that the first and foremost attribute of a good leader is courage. For example, the leader needs to examine the life of David and his encounter with Goliath (1 Sam. 17). The leader will discover incidents in David's life when he demonstrated courage. Additionally, consider the life of Daniel. **Work through the book of Daniel**

and find all the places where Daniel was called to be courageous, listing them in your notebook. The leader will be called to be courageous when conflicts and persecutions come. Further, compare Daniel's story with that of Peter in Mark 14:66-72. The leader that does not have courage will make great concessions in the areas of theology, ethics, values and morals. Failure to speak out on these areas is akin to embracing them. There is a movement afoot to relegate more and more theological issues to being non-essentials. A clear example of this movement is in the area of eschatology. Many churches and mission organizations embrace only the truth that Christ is coming again. The pretribulation rapture and the premillennial return of Christ are considered non-essentials. One reason being given is that these views are not popular with young pastors coming out of many seminaries. The leader must understand that they cannot sacrifice what they believe for acceptance or popularity. **Write a personal basic doctrinal statement.**

- Principle #13: Conflict can be constructive. Many illustrations could be given that would demonstrate the destructiveness of some conflict situations. That being said, wise leaders can turn many conflict situations into moments for ministry. If the leader is not familiar with *Leading Across Cultures: Effective Ministry and Mission in the Global Church* by James Plueddemann and *Caring Enough to Confront: How to Understand and Express Your Deepest Feelings to Others* by David Augsburger, they will need to read these books or find summaries of them on the internet. In Plueddemann's book, the leader should familiarize themselves with high-context and low-context concepts within different cultures as they relate to relationships and leadership building. In Augsburger's book, the leader should understand the five different styles for dealing with conflict (9/9 third way-joint creativity, 9/1 my way-force, 1/9 your way-yield, 1/1 no way-avoidance and 5/5 our way-fifty/fifty). **Examine and delineate the good things that came out of the conflicts in Acts 15:1-35, 36-41.**

- Principle #14: Understanding the gospel story is critical to a strong church planting ministry. **Develop three study outlines explaining the gospel story (justification, sanctification and glorification) as found on page 24 in the main body of this paper. Pay special attention to correctly defining the gospel.**

Application #3: 1 Thessalonians 2:3-6

- Principle #15: Pure motives in ministry must be maintained. This a very crucial subject in the genuineness of the leader. If motives are not scrutinized periodically, they can become very self-fulfilling. According to Paul, this can show itself in error, uncleanliness and deceit. As the leader, analyze impure motives which may occur in future ministry. The leader will notice that Paul, in this text, is very concerned that impure motives do lead to an erroneous gospel. **List the impure motives that Paul reveals in 1 Thessalonians 2:3-6.**

- Principle #16: Leaders have been approved by God to be entrusted with the gospel. The leader needs to have clear understanding of what it means to be entrusted with the gospel. At this point, the leader should write a short paper explaining what it means to be entrusted with the gospel. **Observe that Paul does not leave this subject of the gospel until the leader realizes its extreme importance.**

- Principle #17: It is paramount that the leader be a God pleaser, not a man pleaser. This is not to say many believers will not be pleased with their ministry, however, at times they will teach hard issues which the Holy Spirit uses to convict believers. This teaching will not always please those being taught. This will especially be evident as the leader preaches/teaches the whole counsel of God. After all, the leader must remember it is God who tests the heart. Paul reminded Timothy to "Preach the word! Be ready in season *and* out of season. Convince, rebuke, exhort, with all longsuffering and teaching" (2 Tim. 4:2) The leader cannot be selective about what they preach. They must preach the complete counsel of God!

- Principle #18: Leaders should not use words of flattery for the purpose of manipulating. This principle speaks to the issue of transparency. Paul did not have hidden agendas. He taught the believers of their security in Christ but not freedom from problems and difficulties. Ministering in the majority world necessitates that new believers understand they may be susceptible to persecution. Who can prepare for persecution? Only God can prepare the believer's heart. **Prepare three teaching lessons on persecution from 1 Peter.**

- Principle #19: Never cast an avaricious eye on what belongs to somebody else. This can especially happen when the leader's converts or followers are wealthy, attractive, or influential. A jealous attitude can lead to a covetous lifestyle that may cause the leader to sacrifice their integrity. Jesus told his disciples, "No one can serve two masters; for either he will hate the one and love the other, or else he will be loyal to the one and despise the other. You cannot serve God and mammon" (Matt. 6:24). Paul called this idolatry. "Therefore put to death your members which are on the earth...covetousness, which is idolatry" (Col. 3:5). Also, he warned Timothy, "For the love of money is a root of all *kinds of* evil, for which some have strayed from the faith in their greediness, and pierced themselves through with many sorrows" (1 Tim. 6:10). **Identify your greatest temptation in the area of covetousness and make it a daily matter of prayer. Remember, Paul calls this a "cloak" which indicates it is something that can be concealed. So, be on guard!**

- Principle #20: Glory belongs to God alone. The leader must not be motivated by the desire to acquire a good reputation either from their converts or from outsiders. The leader should allow God to take care of their reputation. If the leader lives a holy life, their reputation will be intact. **Observe what happened to an ancient leader (king) who took upon himself the glory that belonged to God, Dan. 4. Identify and list the statements that Nebuchadnezzar made of himself that in truth belonged to God and to Him alone.**

- Principle #21: Because of the leader's position, authority or power must not be demanded. Paul was an apostle and he could have demanded both authority and power among the believers at Thessalonica but he chose not to. When the leader has a "demanding" attitude they develop a spirit of arrogance rather than a spirit of humility. The leader needs to develop and understand how arrogance and humility are revealed in the life of the leader. Always remember, *"God resists the proud, but gives grace to the humble"* (1Pet. 5:5b italics is mine). **Do a one page word study on "humility".**

Applications #4: 1 Thessalonians 2:7-12

- Principle #22: Have a gentle leadership style. There is no place for heavy-handed leadership. The leader must be "gentle"! Many reading this work will be church planters in the majority world. Their converts will be babes in Christ and will be fragile. Therefore, to develop gentleness the leader must be patient, tenderhearted, respectful, accepting and loyal. Remember, these new believers will struggle with areas in their lives where the leader has found victory. The leader needs to be concerned with those areas of their own life that does not develop gentleness and with God's help eliminate those areas. **What areas of concern need to be eliminated in your leadership style?**

- Principle #23: Be prepared to cherish/nourish all believers, especially new believers. Whether Paul was writing about the natural mother or a wet nurse the imagery is the same. The woman would nurse, care, even at times educate the child. Many children when they became adults, because of the wet nurse's gentleness and love, would free the wet nurse from her slavery. Using this imagery, the role of the leader is clear. They need to study the Word so it can be passed on in simple lessons to the new believer, just like a mother eats and passes on the nourishing milk to her infant. The leader needs to be proficient in the discipleship process. Leaders are commissioned not only to "preach the gospel" (Mark 16:15), but also to "make disciples" (Matt. 28:19). **Read five commands of your choice in the book *A Weekly Discipleship Journal: 52 Commands of Christ*, written by the author of this paper. (see bibliography)**

- Principle #24: Have heartfelt love for the ones being served. Some say these words "affectionately longing" are words of endearment derived from the nursey, cf. p.42, footnote 72. As the church plant grows, the leader may develop an impersonal relationship with their flock and if this happens the discipleship ministry, as well, will become impersonal. This causes the discipleship process to become a class once a week that is more academic than practical. As leaders are developed, one area where they need to be efficient is the art of making disciples. Making disciples may be the major ministry of leaders in a growing church. The leader needs to follow a clearly defined discipleship plan. **Review your discipleship plan, making any adjustments you believe to be necessary.** Remember, the plan must have a component that demonstrates a loving concern for the new believer. This will probably be developed through a one-on-one relationship.

- Principle #25: Don't just impart the gospel, give teaching to everyone but especially the new believers. It is necessary for the leader to find ways to demonstrate transparency to the ones they serve. Many majority world cultures are high context cultures (caring more for relationships than task). This means spending time with new believers is critical, requiring learning their language, eating their food, drinking their coffee (some Ethiopians put rancid butter and salt in their coffee) and listening to their stories. Many traditions are passed on by means of narrative. Many times a narrative will show the heart of the people. This time spent with the people will help the leader know how to contextualize the gospel so it has meaning within a particular culture. **Develop a time log to know how much time is actually being spent in face-to-face discipling encounters.**

- Principle #26: Leadership is hard work! Paul and his companions worked hard, "...labor and toil; for our laboring night and day..." (1 Thess. 2:9a). Acts 18:3 records, like the Corinthians, they were tentmakers - "for by occupation they were tentmakers". The point is when commencing a new ministry, like planting a church, the leader must be supported by the sending church or by their own employment. The leader cannot become a burden to a new struggling ministry. If the leader is expecting too much financial support from the new believers, it could be misunderstood and prohibit the preaching of the gospel. The launching of a new ministry must focus on the preaching of the death, burial and resurrection of Christ. For this to happen the leader may be called upon to sacrifice greatly. This will require budgeting their finances carefully. **Fill out a budget form before going to a ministry or shortly thereafter.**

- Principle #27: Leadership requires Christ-like behavior. Paul declares before God and the Thessalonian believers that he and his missionary team had behaved in a Christ-like manner. They were devout, just and blameless. **Review the comments made on verse 10, cf. pages 47-49 in the main body of this paper, and be able to describe what you believe and what it means to you.** The ability to lead can be destroyed quickly if the leader's walk does not coincide with his talk.

- Principle #28: Challenge children in the faith to "walk worthy of God". **After reviewing the comments made on verses 11-12 on pages 49-53 add to your discipleship plan, including the concepts of "exhort", "comfort", and "charge". Be sure you understand the implications of these three words.** The leader should not let time lapse between individuals coming to Christ and the beginning of the discipleship process.

NOTEBOOK

NOTEBOOK

NOTEBOOK

NOTEBOOK

NOTEBOOK

NOTEBOOK

NOTEBOOK

NOTEBOOK

NOTEBOOK

NOTEBOOK

APPENDIX #2: TEACHING SERMONS ON 1 THESSALONIANS 1 & 2

HOMILETICAL OUTLINE: THE MODEL CHURCH
I THESSALONIANS 1:1-8 [PART#1]

Introduction: 1Th. 1:1 "Paul, Silvanus, and Timothy, To the church of the Thessalonians in God the Father and the Lord Jesus Christ: Grace to you and peace from God our Father and the Lord Jesus Christ."

1. **The City:**

   a. Location-major city in Macedonia
   b. Founded: 315 B.C. by Cassander named after his wife, the stepsister of Alexander the Great.
   c. Prominence:

      1) Capital of Macedonia
      2) Second largest city in the area second only to Philippi
      3) On a "freeway" Via Egnatia Cicero: "lying in the lap of the empire"
      4) Free city= had its own government, ruled by politarchs.

    d. Inhabitants: Greeks & small Jewish community.

2. **The Church:**

    a. Origin: second missionary journey, **Acts 17:1-10**
    b. Membership: started in a synagogue. "Jews, God-fearing Greek, not a few prominent women"
    c. Tenure: three weeks in synagogue [longer ministry outside the city, **cf. 1Thess. 2:9; Phil. 4:15,16**]
    d. Opposition: **Acts 17:5-9**
    e. Occasion: Paul had sent Timothy to bring back a report. **cp. Chapter 3.**

      1) To record the writers' joy at the good news
      2) To refute false charges against his ministry.

3) To remind them of biblical values and doctrines that needed to be reviewed **cf. 1Thess. 4:9; 5:1**

f. Place & date: Corinth c. 51 A.D.

3. **Greeting:** "grace" [Gk: to rejoice], "peace" [Heb: prosperity]

a. Writers: Paul [**2Cor.10:10**], Silas, Timothy.
b. Readers: the church at Thessalonica, assembly: called out ones.

1) "In God the Father": distinguishes it from any pagan assembly.
2) "In the Lord Jesus Christ" distinguishes it from any Jewish assembly.

**WHAT MADE THIS CHURCH A MODEL ASSEMBLY OF BELIEVERS?

I. **THE CHARACTER OF HIS COMMENDATION, I Thess. 1:2. "We give thanks to God always for you all, making mention of you in our prayers,"**

A. <u>Practice</u>: "always" thanking God for them, **1Thess. 1:2**

1. There is always something we can be thankful for in others.
2. This was a word of encouragement.

Ill: It is told that once the Duke of Wellington's cook gave notice and left him. He was asked why he had left so honorable and well-paid a position. His answer was, "When the dinner is good, the Duke never praises me and when it is bad, he never blames me; it was just not worth while."[103]

B. <u>Prayer</u>: **1thess. 1:2a** They prayed together. **"prayer, petition, praise with thanksgiving"**

C. <u>Persistence</u>: "continually remember..." **1Thess. 1:2b**

II. THE CHARACTERISTICS OF THIS CHURCH, I Thess. 1:3-8.

A. <u>Their work produced by faith</u>. **1Thess 1:3a,4-5. 1Thess. 1:3a "remembering without ceasing your work of faith..." 1Thess.1:4 knowing, beloved brethren, your election by God. 1Thess.1:5 For our gospel did not come to you in word only, but also in power, and in the Holy Spirit and in much assurance, as you know what kind of men we were among you for your sake.**

　　1. **"Beloved" 1Thess 1:4a "knowing, beloved (loved by God) brethren"** love in the past existing into the present.
　　2. Chosen by God, **1Thess. 1:4a "your election by God."**

3. Saved by God, **1Thess. 1:5 "For our gospel did not come to you in word only, but also in power, and in the Holy Spirit and in much assurance, as you know what kind of men we were among you for your sake."**

Gospel not but with word
    in power
        in Holy Spirit
    in deep conviction

Ill: How do you know you are one of the elect? Respond to the Gospel and you are one of the elect

B. <u>Their labor prompted by love</u>. **1Thess 1:3b,8**

1Thess. 1:3b "remembering without ceasing your labor of love…"

1. sounded out by labor and love. (echoing like thunder or sounding out as a trumpet)

1Thess. 1:8a "For from you the word of the Lord has sounded forth, not only in Macedonia and Achaia…"

2. spread out by labor and love.

1Thess. 1:8b "but also in every place. Your faith toward God has gone out, so that we do not need to say anything."

C. <u>Their endurance inspired by hope</u>, **1Thess. 1:3c,6-7.**

> **"remembering without ceasing your patience of hope in our Lord Jesus Christ in the sight of our God and Father."**

1. Imitators of the Apostles and the Lord.

   > **1Thess. 1:6a "And you became followers of us and of the Lord..."**

2. Joyous by the Holy Spirit (originating cause)

   > **1Thess. 1:6b "having received the word in much affliction, with joy of the Holy Spirit..."**

3. Models to others.
   > "mark" - A mark left by a blow an example to the model church.
   > **1Thess. 1:7 "so that you became examples to all in Macedonia and Achaia who believe."**

CONCLUSION:

1. These Christians were made of the right stuff.
2. They had commitment to God, service, and waiting!

HOMILETICAL OUTLINE:
THE MODEL CHURCH
I THESSALONIANS 1:9,10 [PART #2]

[Review] WHAT MADE THIS CHURCH A MODEL ASSEMBLY OF BELIEVERS?

1. **THE CHARACTERISTICS OF THIS CHURCH, 1Thess. 1:3-8.**

    + Their work of faith. **1Thess. 1:3a,4-5.**
    + Their labor of love. **1Thess. 1:3b,8**
    + Their patience of hope, **1Thess. 1:3c,6-7.**

2. **THE CONDUCT OF THIS CHURCH, I Thess. 1:9-10.**

    1Thess. 1:9a "For they themselves [both Christians & heathen] declare concerning us what manner of entry we had to you…"

I. **CONFIRMED FAITH, v:9b "…turned to God from Idols…"**

A. Positive: **"…how you turned to God…" to serve the living and true God**

    1. "turned" (Aorist) - This is the regular word for conversion-to turn around.
    2. "to face to face" relationship with God

B. Negative: **"from Idols"** (away from)

> (Truth cannot co-exist with error)
> **salvation doesn't begin with giving up something but with receiving someone!

1. This phrase indicates that most of the believers were Gentiles not Jews.
2. "from" means a permanent turning

II. **CONFIRMED LOVE, 1Thess.1:9c "...to serve the living and the true God,"**

> (to serve. pre/inf. continuous, complete, whole-hearted service to God. "to serve as a slave")

A. "living" - "He has risen he has risen indeed" This is in contrast to the dead idols.
B. "true" - genuine, real in contrast to counterfeit gods of idolatry.

III. **CONFIRMED HOPE, 1Thess. 1:10. "...to wait for his son..."**

A. The Character of their Hope: Patience wait-up for His Son (present tense)
B. The Content of their Hope: Person

> **"...his Son from heaven, whom he raised from the dead —Jesus..."**

1. "his Son" (deity)
2. "Jesus" (humanity)

C. The Center of their Hope: Deliverance.

   1. **"who [is] rescuing us..."**
   2. "...from the coming wrath."

Conclusion:

1. A model church is characterized by faith, love, hope.
2. May our church also be characterized by these three characteristics.
3. This year, look for opportunities to but these three characteristics into practices.

HOMILETICAL OUTLINE: THE MODEL LEADER I THESSALONIANS 2:1-12

Introduction: The definitions of a leader:

1. "Inspiring influence". Those who lead others with the greatest degree of success are able to light the spark that prompts others toward co-operation, hard work, and if necessary, personal sacrifice."   -C. Swindoll
2. "A leader is someone who knows where he's going and can get others to follow him." -Howard Hendricks
3. Hendricks definitions is:
   > *goal oriented: the leader knows where he is going
   >
   > *people oriented: the leader can motivate others to follow him
4. Leadership styles differ but qualities of a leader that are spelled out in our passage this morning do not change.

I. THE MANNER OF A LEADER, I THESS. 2:1,2 (Historically)

A. <u>Productive</u>, **"not in vain" empty, failure. 1Thess. 2:1 "For You yourselves know, brethren that our coming unto you was not in vain."**

B. <u>Proclamation</u>, **"to speak...the gospel." 1Thess. 2:2 "But even after we had suffered before**

and were spitefully treated at Philippi, as you know, we were bold in our God to speak to you the gospel of God…"

C. Persistent, **"in much conflict." 1Thess. 2:2.**

> physical
> spitefully treated-public humiliation
> in much conflict place in a race or contest

II. THE MOTIVES OF A LEADER, I THESS.2:3-6 (Things to omit)

A. Prevarication, **1Thess. 2:3 "For our exhortation *did* not *come* from error or uncleanness, nor *was it* in deceit."**

1. "from error" "the leading astray"
2. "uncleanness" "out of impure motives",
3. "in deceit" "in trickery" : a bait or trap (subject: INTEGRITY)

B. People-pleasing, **1Thess. 2:4 "But as we have been approved by God to be entrusted with the gospel, even so we speak, not as pleasing men, but God who tests our hearts." (peace at any price)**

1. approved by God outward his ministry was tested
   - 3 years in isolation-Arabia
   - 7 years in Tarsus
   - 1st missionary Journey

-disappointment J. Mark
-danger- stoned
*Inward his ministry was tested
(subject: endorsement)

2. "approved by men" This will not always happen. (be affirmed as a leader!)

C. <u>Piggishness</u>, **1Thess. 2:5 "For neither at any time did we use flattering words, as you know, nor a cloak for covetousness—God *is* witness."**

1. No flattery "to win the heart to exploit them" Lightfoot.
2. No mask "cloak, cover up"
   They were real people-transparency.

D. <u>Praise-seeking</u>, **1Thess. 2:6a "Nor did we seek glory from men, either from you or from others…"**
   **divine approval not public esteem

E. <u>Position-hungry</u>, **v1Thess. 2:6b "…when we might have made demands as apostles of Christ."**
   **They did not use their position as Apostles to get authority. The right to rule is earned for a leader never demanded!

III. THE MODEL OF A LEADER. I THESS. 2:7-12
(Things to include)

A. <u>Attending to People</u>, 1Thess. 2:7 "But we were gentle among you, just as a nursing *mother* cherishes her own children."

 1. Gentle not authoritarian
 2. Protection not position
 3. Providing not piggishness
    caring-to warm, to foster, to nourish, to cherish. [Deut.22:6 LXX bird warming her eggs.]

B. <u>Affection for People</u>, 1Thess. 2:8a "So, affectionately longing for you..." cp. Job 3:21LXX word of endearment from the nursery. ("to be attached to") He did not see men as trees walking.

C. <u>Authentic before People</u>, 1Thess. 2:8b-10 "we were well pleased to impart to you not only the gospel of God, but also our own lives, because you had become dear to us."
1Thess. 2:9 "For you remember, brethren, our labor and toil; for laboring night and day, that we might not be a burden to any of you, we preached to you the gospel of God."
1Thess. 2:10 "You *are* witnesses, and God *also*, how devoutly and justly and blamelessly we behaved ourselves among you who believe."

"They shared"

1. The Gospel, **1Thess. 2:8b.**
2. Their lives also, **1Thess. 2:8c-10**

   a. worked-toil, hardship
   b. witnessed-preached the gospel
   c. walked-holy, righteous, blameless

D. <u>**Affirmation of People**</u>, **vv:11-12 1Thess. 2:11**
   "as you know how we exhorted, and comforted, and charged every one of you, as a father *does* his own children"
   1Thess. 2:12 "that you would walk worthy of God who calls you into His own kingdom and glory."
   (e.g. like a father)

1. encouraging
   "to exhort to a particular line of conduct"
      **Principle
2. Comforting "to encourage to continue in a course"
      **Persistence
3. Urging "to urge a person to walk in God's ways"
      **Practice

Conclusion: This will produce four qualities (summary).

1. Truthfulness, **1Thess. 2:3**
2. Transparency, **1Thess. 2:5**

3. Touch, **1Thess. 2**:7
4. Trust, **1Thess. 2**:13

---

[103] William Barclay, *The Letters to the Philippians, Colossians, and Thessalonians.* (Philadelphia: The Westminster Press, 1959), 186.

BIBLIOGRAPHY

GENERAL STUDIES:

Accordance Bible Study Software for the Macintosh 10.4.3. OakTree Software Inc. (www.acordancebible.com), 2014.

Augsburger, David. *Caring Enough to Confront,* Grand Rapids: Revell, *2009.*

Clinton, Arnold E. *Zondervan Illustrated Bible Backgrounds Commentary, Vol. 3.* Grand Rapids: Zondervan, 2002.

Conybeare, W.J. and Howson, J.S. *The Life and Epistles of St. Paul.* Grand Rapids: Wm. B. Eerdmans Publishing Company, 1978.

Hiebert, D. Edmond, *An Introduction to the Pauline Epistles,* Chicago: Moody Press, 1954.

Jusu, John, Supervising Editor, *Africa Study Bible* Wheaton: Oasis International Ltd, 2016.

McKnight, Scot. *The Jesus Creed,* Paraclete Press: Brewster, 2004

Plueddemann, James E. *Leading Across Cultures,* Downers Grove: IVP Academic, 2009.

Shepard, J.W. *The Life and Letters of St. Paul.* Grand Rapids: Wm. B. Eerdmans Publishing Company, 1950.

TOPICAL WORKS:

Badger, Anthony B. *Confronting Calvinism.* Lexington: Self Published by Author 2013.

Bettenson, Henry. *Documents of the Christian Church.* London: Oxford University Press, 1963.

DeBeor, Willis Peter. *The Imitation of Paul. An Exegetical Study.* Kampem: J.H. Kok, 1962.

Esterline Sr., Dan A. *A Weekly Discipleship Journal 52 Commands of Christ.* Wausau: DigiCopy, 2003.

Hixson, J.B., Whitmire, Rick, Zuck, Roy B. *Freely By His Grace: Classical Free Grace Theology.* Duluth: Grace Gospel Press, 2012.

Klein, William W. *The New Chosen People.* Grand Rapids: Acadmie Books Zondervan Publishing House, 1990.

Murray, Andrew. *WITH CHRIST In the School of Prayer.* New York: Fleming H. Revell Company, 1885.

Telford, Andrew. *Subjects of Sovereignty.* Orlando: The Daniels Publishers, N.D.

GREEK STUDIES:

Aland, Barbara, Aland, Kurd, Johannes Karvidopoulos, Johannes, Martini, Carlo M. and Metzger, Bruce M. *The Greek New Testament 4th Edition.* Stuttgart: United Bible Societies, 1994.

Hodges, Zane C. and Farstad, Arthur L. (Editors)*The Greek New Testament According to the Majority Text*. Nashville: Thomas Nelson Publishers, 1982.

Jongkind, Dirk, (Editor) *The Greek New Testament*. Wheaton: Crossway, 2017.

Nestle, Erwin and Aland, Kurt. *The Greek New Testament Nestle-Aland Novum Testamentum Graece 27th edition*. Stuttgart: Deutsche Biblelgesellschaft (United Bible Societies, 2001.

Moulton, James Hope and Moulton, George. *The Vocabulary of the Greek New Testament*. London: Hodder & Stoughton, 1952.

Mounce, William D. *Basics of Biblical Greek*. Grand Rapids: Zondervan Publishing House, 1993.

Rogers Jr., Cleon L. & Rogers III, Cleon L. *The New Linguistic and Exegetical Key to the Greek New Testament*. Grand Rapids: Zondervan Publishing House, 1998.

Summer, Ray and Sawyer. *Essentials of New Testament Greek*. Nashville: Broadman & Holman Publishers, 1995.

Wallace Daniel B. *The Basics of New Testament Syntax*. Grand Rapids: Zondervan Publishing House, 2000.

_____ *Greek Grammar Beyond the Basics*. Grand Rapids: Zondervan Publishing House, 1996.

Walvoord, John E. & Zuck, Roy B. (Editors) *The Bible Knowledge Commentary New Testament.*, Colorado Springs: Victor (Cook Communications Ministries), 2000.

Wilkin, Robert N. *The Grace New Testament Commentary Volume 2: Romans-Revelation*. Edited by Denton, TX: Grace Evangelical Society, 2010.

COMMENTARIES:

Barclay, William. *The Letters to the Philippians, Colossians, and Thessalonians*. Philadelphia: The Westminster Press, 1959.

Beale, G.K. *1-2 Thessalonians*. Downers Grove: IVP Academic, 2003.

Blight, Richard C. *An Exegetical Summary of 1 & 2 Thessalonians*. Dallas: International Press, 1989.

Fee, Gordon D. *The First and Second Letters to the Thessalonians*. Grand Rapids: William B. Eerdmans Publishing Company, 2009.

Findlay, George G. *Cambridge Greek Testament, The Epistles of Paul the Apostle to the Thessalonians*. Cambridge: U. Press, 1904.

Green, Gene L. *The Letters to the Thessalonians*. Grand Rapids: William B. Eerdmans Publishing Company, 2002.

Hiebert, D. Edmond. *The Thessalonian Epistle*. Chicago: Moody Press, 1971.

Hogg, C.F. & Vine, W.E. *the Epistles to the Thessalonians*. Fincastle: Scripture Truth Book Company, 1959.

Lenski, R.C.H. *The Interpretation of St. Paul's Epistles to the Colossians, to the Thessalonians, to Timothy, to Titus and to Philemon*. Minneapolis: Augsburg Publishing House, 1964.

Lightfoot, J.B. *Saint Paul's Epistles to the Colossians and to Philemon*. Grand Rapids: Zondervan Publishing House, 1968.

Lünemann, Gottlieb. *Meyer's Critical and Exegetical Commentary on the New Testament*. Edinburgh: T. & T. Clark, 1884.

McKnight, Scott. *The Story of God Bible Commentary: Sermon on the Mount*. Zondervan: Grand Rapids, 2013.

Moffatt, James "The First and Second Epistles to the Thessalonians." in *The Expositor's Greek Testament, volume IV*, ed. Nicoll, Robertson W. Peabody, Mass.: Hendrickson Publishers, 2002.

Robertson, Archibald Thomas. *Word Pictures in the New Testament, Volume IV The Epistles of Paul*. Nashville: Broadman Press, 1931.

Rydelink, Michael & Vanlandingham, Michael (General Editors). *The Moody Bible Commentary*. Chicago: MoodyPublisher, 2014.

Ryrie, Charles Caldwell. *First & Second Thessalonians*. Chicago: Moody Press, 1959.

Walvoord, John F. and Hitchcock, Mark. *1 & 2 Thessalonians*. Chicago: Moody Publishers, 2012.

Wiersbe, Warren W. *The Wiersbe Bible Commentary, New Testament*. Colorado Springs: David C. Cook, 2007.

Wright, N.T. *Paul for Everyone, Galatians and Thessalonians*. Louisville: Westminster John Knox Press, 2004.

CLASS NOTES:

Haik, Paul. *Greek Exegesis I & II Thessalonians*. Chicago: Moody Bible Institute, 1962.

Printed in the United States
By Bookmasters